'Tis the SEASON to Be FELT-Y

KATHY SHELDON

with

AMANDA CARESTIO

LARK

New York

LARK
New York

An Imprint of Sterling Publishing
1166 Avenue of the Americas
New York, NY 10036

Text © 2015 by Kathy Sheldon
Photography & illustrations © 2015 by Lark Crafts

Photography by Susan Wasinger
Illustrations by Orrin Lundgren

ISBN 978-1-4547-0886-5

Distributed in Canada by Sterling Publishing
c/o Canadian Manda Group, 664 Annette Street
Toronto, Ontario, Canada M6S 2C8
Distributed in the United Kingdom by GMC Distribution Services
Castle Place, 166 High Street, Lewes, East Sussex, England BN7 1XU
Distributed in Australia by Capricorn Link (Australia) Pty. Ltd.
P.O. Box 704, Windsor, NSW 2756, Australia

For information about custom editions, special sales, and premium and corporate purchases, please
contact Sterling Special Sales at 800-805-5489 or specialsales@sterlingpublishing.com.

Manufactured in China

2 4 6 8 10 9 7 5 3 1

larkcrafts.com

Contents

Introduction

AFTER "HAPPY HOLIDAYS!" THE NEXT thing we want to say is a great big "Thank you!" for the wonderful reception to our first felt holiday book, *Fa la la la Felt!* That collection of felt Christmas projects was our pet project (and our first collaboration). It's been heart-warming to see the adorable projects so many of you have made from that now very popular book.

Your chorus of more, more, more has been heard loud and clear, so here it is: 40-plus new projects to celebrate the season from many of the same awesomely talented designers we featured in *Fa la la la Felt*. Because felt (unlike woven fabrics) does not fray when cut, it is one of the easiest materials to use, and yet, because it comes in so many different delicious colors and types (from polyester to bamboo to pure wool), it's beloved by beginning sewers (even children!) and experienced designers, alike. That makes it the perfect material to use at what is, for most of us, the busiest time of year. The Felt Basics, starting on the facing page, will provide a quick primer if you're new to felt, including a handy reference for embroidery stitches starting on page 10.

Whether you want to add a handmade touch to your tree this year or you're looking for a way to add quick color to your mantle before a holiday party, the projects in this book are going to make your season merry and bright. If your decorating style leans toward elegant neutrals, the Dove Ornaments on page 22 will appeal to you. If the jolly holidays tempt you toward kitsch, check out the Kool Kristmas Kitty on page 28 or our mod Bird Mobile on page 52. Pair the Cocoa Coasters (page 108) with some hot chocolate mix for a sweet handmade gift, or if you really want to bring a smile to someone's face, sew the adorable Happy Elf Friends on page 105. Santa will get a kick out of filling any of the stockings in the book, whether you choose the Caroling Bird Stocking (page 102) or the cowgirl in you chooses the Western Stocking (page 100).

We're so happy to share these wonderful new projects from talented and generous designers. Putting aside some quiet time to create is a great way to slow down the rush of Christmas. 'Tis the season to get felt-y!

Felt Basics

Here's a quick refresher on the materials, tools, and techniques needed to make the projects in this book. But relax—there's a reason we get all fa la la la about felt: felt makes crafting easy! And improvising is definitely allowed. Feel free to use fabric glue in place of stitching if you think it will work as well and you're in a hurry or working with children. Substitute an embroidery stitch you know if the one called for intimidates you. The point here is not just to make adorable things with felt, but also to enjoy the process of making!

Materials & Tools

We'll wager that if you've done any sewing at all, you already have (and know) much of what's needed to make the projects in this book. Look at the Basic Sewing Kit (page 7) and then skim the What You Need list before beginning a project. A number of the projects call for embroidery stitches: You'll find a guide to all of them starting on page 10.

FELT

Every time we visit a craft or fabric store, browse Etsy, or head to the many other online suppliers of felt, we're floored by both the luscious colors and the many new varieties of felt. When we wrote *Fa la la la Felt*, felt was just starting to overcome its reputation as the stuff Grandma used to make tacky Christmas crafts.

Fast-forward to today, and the felt section of most fabric and craft stores (or online shops) has a range of colors and felt types that's almost overwhelming. You can find 100 percent wool felt, wool/rayon felt, acrylic felt, eco felt made from post-consumer recycled plastic bottles, felt made from bamboo and rayon, felt with adhesive backing, and felt embedded with sparkles. It comes in sheets (usually known as craft felt) or as yardage and in solid colors and playful patterns.

WOOL FELT   One hundred percent wool is the thickest and sturdiest felt. It usually comes in beautiful, subtle (and often hand-dyed) colors. It won't tear apart or pill the way acrylic felt sometimes does. Wool felt is more expensive than acrylic or wool blend felt, and it's harder to find at big craft stores, but you can find pure wool felt online. Because of the cost, we tend to save our 100 percent wool felt for smaller, special projects.

WOOL BLEND FELT   Wool blend felt is similar to 100 percent wool felt and comes in many of the same warm, subtle colors. The addition of synthetic fibers makes the felt more flexible, so it's easier to sew and drapes a little better than pure wool felt. Wool blend felt costs less than wool felt but more than acrylic felt. If you can't find wool blend felt at your local craft or fabric store, you can purchase it online, but beware: the color choices are so fantastic that you'll want to buy a little of everything!

ACRYLIC FELT   Acrylic felt (sold in both sheets and as yardage) is made by pressing tiny acrylic fibers together until they interlock into a mat of material. It's inexpensive, widely available, and fade resistant. But acrylic felt is usually thinner—and therefore more transparent—than wool or wool blend felt. This kind of felt is fine for most projects, but it can stretch out of shape and open up at seams and stitch holes

Creating Felted Fabric

Felting fabric is easy; in fact, you've probably done it before when you've accidentally put a wool sweater through a laundry cycle. Here's how to do it on purpose:

1. Start with a 100 percent wool garment. Crafters typically use wool sweaters, but wool slacks, blazers, and winter coats also create beautiful felted fabric (take a look at Lisa Jordan's Partridge & Pears Ornaments above and on page 30).

2. Remove any liners, zippers, buttons, etc., from your item, and then place it in a zippered lingerie bag or a pillow protector (to prevent wet lint from clogging up your washing machine).

3. Set your washer to the hot wash/cold rinse cycle, and use the lowest water level setting and the longest cycle. Add about one tablespoon of mild dish soap or wool wash.

4. If the material shrinks as desired, hang it to dry. If you want more shrinkage, wash it again and then dry it in your dryer. The end result should be soft felted fabric that won't ravel when cut. If you'd like, use a sweater shaver to de-fuzz it and a steam iron to remove any wrinkles.

(especially in stuffed projects or projects subject to a lot of stress), and gets fuzzy if handled a lot. We've found that as felt has become more popular and widely available, the quality of acrylic felt has also started to vary greatly, so hold each sheet or bolt of felt up to the light and examine it before buying—felt that's so thin that it's transparent won't work well for some projects.

ECO FELT   Made from post-consumer plastic bottles, eco felt shares almost all of acrylic felt's characteristics. You can find eco felt in most crafts stores as well as online, and you probably won't notice a big difference between it and acrylic felt. One added benefit of acrylic and eco felt is that people who are allergic to wool or are averse to using products that come from animals prefer to craft with them.

BAMBOO FELT   Bamboo felt is typically 50 percent bamboo and 50 percent rayon. This makes it a very soft, natural material that is also vegan. If you can't find bamboo felt at your local craft store, look online.

STIFFENED FELT   This felt, which comes in both 12 x 18-inch (30.5 cm x 45.7 cm) and 9 x 12-inch (22.9 x 30.5 cm) sheets, is extra stiff, which makes it great for projects like the Polar Bear Gift Bag (page 114) or the Teeter Tots (page 46). You can find it in most large craft stores and online.

ADHESIVE-BACKED FELT   Adhesive-backed felt sheets come in handy for some no-sew projects or to add details to stitched projects. The sticky stuff on the back of these felt sheets can gunk up scissors or needles used to cut or pierce the felt. A quick swipe from a cotton ball dipped in nail polish remover should take care of the problem.

WOOL ROVING   Wool roving is carded wool drawn into long continuous strands and is used for needle felting. Needle felting (also referred to as "felting") is a method of sculpting shapes from wool roving by jabbing the fibers with a barbed needle until they bind together and become dense. If you want to give it a try, the Mistletoe Sprig (page 74) and Bird Mobile (page 52) call for simple felt balls you can needle felt easily (see page 9). Of course, you can also cheat and buy felt balls in the felt section of many craft stores. As felting has become more popular, wool roving is getting easier to find online and in many craft stores.

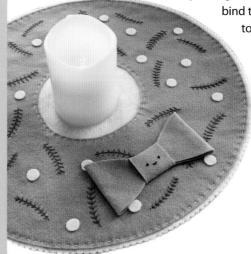

THREAD AND EMBROIDERY FLOSS

You know how there are some things where it really does pay to spend a bit more for the better stuff? That's true for thread. Use a quality polyester, cotton/polyester blend, or all-cotton thread for the projects that require machine or hand stitching. It will make your sewing both easier and more professional looking, and it will create seams that hold up.

Because felt and embroidery go together so well, you'll notice a fair number of projects with embroidery in this book. Embroidery floss is available in just about every shade of every color you can imagine at craft and fabric stores. (And it costs so little it's hard not to buy it by the handful!) A strand of embroidery floss is usually made up of six individual threads twisted together. Many projects call for using just two or three of the strands. To separate strands without a tangled mess, hold the ends of the number of strands desired, and then very slowly pull these away from the rest of the threads in the strand.

STUFFING

Polyester fiberfill, cotton batting, wool roving, or sewing scraps can be used to stuff projects. The Clove-Filled Orange Pomander Ornaments on page 18 are stuffed with whole cloves for a delicious scent.

RIBBONS, BUTTONS, BEADS, AND OTHER YUMMY EMBELLISHMENTS

Before you head out for supplies, look at the What You Need list for the projects you want to make, and note any buttons, grommets, ribbon, rickrack, etc., you'll need. Of course, you can feel free to think of the embellishments we've used as suggestions and substitute freely with what you already have on hand. But if you're like us, you'll welcome an excuse to peruse the ribbon, button, or bead section of a shop.

Basic Sewing Kit

scissors

pinking or scallop shears

small embroidery or manicure scissors

rotary cutting tools (optional)

straight pins

hand-sewing and embroidery needles

tissue or tracing paper

freezer paper

embroidery hoop

sewing machine (optional)

iron

ruler

craft glue

fabric glue

disappearing or water-soluble fabric pen

ADHESIVES

Fabric glue, craft glue, tacky glue, permanent spray adhesive, and temporary spray adhesive are called for in some of these projects. If you don't have what's listed, just test whatever adhesive you do have on some felt scraps before substituting.

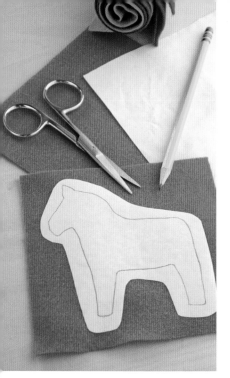

Basic Techniques

We're not kidding about the "basic" part here. Most of the same techniques you use with other sewing projects work fine with felt; in fact, felt is usually easier to work with than other fabrics! We've included a couple of no-sew projects, and if you're in a holiday rush and the instructions say to sew an embellishment onto an ornament but you'd rather use fabric glue, go for it!

TRANSFERRING TEMPLATES AND EMBROIDERY DESIGNS

Templates for all of the projects in this book can be found starting on page 116. Transferring templates and embroidery designs to felt (especially dark colors) can be tricky. Here are some of the techniques we use.

FREEZER PAPER METHOD

One of our favorite ways to transfer templates to felt is with freezer paper and an iron. Freezer paper (available in most supermarkets near the foil and plastic wrap) has a waxy side that, when ironed, allows it to temporarily stick to felt so you can accurately cut out a shape, and then remove the paper without leaving residue behind. It's translucent enough that you can usually trace over a template, just as you would with tracing paper. You can even purchase sheets of freezer paper meant for inkjet printers online. We've had good luck simply cutting our freezer paper to size and taping it (waxy side down) onto a regular sheet of paper and running that through an inkjet printer, but try this in your own inkjet printer at your own risk and do NOT use a laser printer: It will melt the wax and ruin your printer.

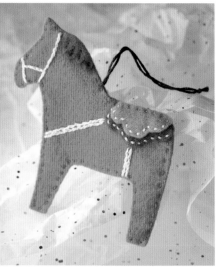

1) Trace the template at the correct size onto the plain (unwaxed) side of the freezer paper (if you can't see through the paper well enough, hold the template and freezer paper against a window to trace). Make sure you are drawing on the unwaxed side of the paper—if you iron the waxy side, you'll have a sticky mess on your iron!

2) Cut roughly around the outside of the traced template, leaving a border of freezer paper.

3) Place the template onto your felt, waxy side down, and use an iron at a low setting with no steam to adhere the template to the felt.

4) Cut along the traced lines to cut out the shape, and then remove the freezer paper.

TISSUE PAPER METHOD

For patterns with embroidery designs, enlarge the template to the appropriate size, and then trace the template (including any embroidery patterns) onto a piece of tissue paper. Pin the tissue paper in place on the felt piece to be embroidered. Embroider the designs (through both the felt and the paper). When finished, cut out the felt shape and tear away the tissue paper. You may need to use a sewing needle or tweezers to pull out any tiny (or as our favorite British designer Laura Howard calls them, "fiddly") pieces of tissue stuck under your stitches.

TRACING METHODS

If you don't have freezer paper, for medium to large pattern pieces in simple shapes, just enlarge the template to the appropriate size and cut it out. Then pin this template onto the felt, and cut around it to cut out the shape. For small or intricate shapes, cut out the paper template, pin it to the felt, and then use a disappearing or water-soluble fabric pen to trace around the template, directly onto the felt. (Test your fabric pen on a piece of scrap felt first—some "disappear" better than others.) Use the traced lines to cut. Disappearing or water-soluble fabric pens can also be used with thin light-colored felt to trace embroidery lines. Just place the felt on top of the pattern and trace the stitch lines with the marker. (For intricate embroidery patterns that may take a while to complete, use a water-soluble fabric marker instead of a disappearing one.)

TO HOOP OR NOT TO HOOP

When you're embroidering small or intricate details on felt, sometimes it's easier to place the felt in an embroidery hoop first, embroider, release the felt, and then cut out the felt shape needed, and sometimes it's easier to skip the hoop and simply cut out the shape and embroider it. Different designers use different methods, so experiment so see which method works best for you with individual projects.

FINISHING FELT

Why do we keep mentioning the fact that felt doesn't fray? Because it means we can avoid most of the fussy aspects of sewing that we don't really enjoy. It also means the edges of your projects can be finished (or not) in all kinds of ways:

- If you love the made-by-hand look, use a straight (or running) stitch (page 10) near the edge of the felt and leave the edges raw (or scalloped) like Mollie Johanson did with her Christmas Is Coming Wreath Mat (page 54).
- There's something super crafty-looking about the blanket stitch. See Laura Howard's Gingerbread Village Ornaments (page 26) for an example and page 10 for instructions for the blanket stitch.
- When a project calls for a polished look, machine stitching around the outside edge of the felt is often what's needed. See the Scrappy Wreath (page 84) for an example.
- Or skip the stitching altogether and just go with cut edges: See the Pretty in Pink Poinsettia Wreath (page 76).

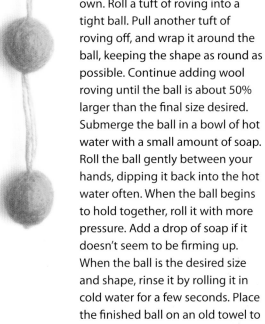

DIY FELT BALLS

You can buy felt balls at craft stores, but if you have wool roving (see page 6), you can easily make your own. Roll a tuft of roving into a tight ball. Pull another tuft of roving off, and wrap it around the ball, keeping the shape as round as possible. Continue adding wool roving until the ball is about 50% larger than the final size desired. Submerge the ball in a bowl of hot water with a small amount of soap. Roll the ball gently between your hands, dipping it back into the hot water often. When the ball begins to hold together, roll it with more pressure. Add a drop of soap if it doesn't seem to be firming up. When the ball is the desired size and shape, rinse it by rolling it in cold water for a few seconds. Place the finished ball on an old towel to dry completely.

Embroidery Stitches

Use these illustrations to help you with any unfamiliar stitches.

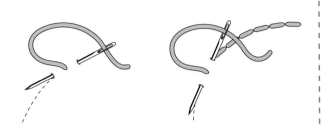

BACKSTITCH   This simple stitch creates a solid line, so it's great for outlining shapes or creating text.

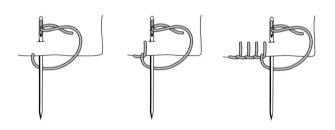

BLANKET STITCH   The blanket stitch is both decorative and functional. Use this stitch to accentuate an edge or to attach an appliqué.

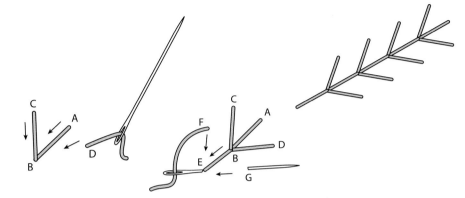

FERN STITCH   The fern stitch consists of three straight stitches that radiate from a central point. Stitch the middle stitch first (this will create the "spine" of the stitch) and then add a straight stitch on either side the middle stitch.

FRENCH KNOT   This elegant little knot adds interest and texture when embroidering or embellishing.

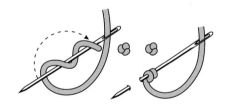

CROSS STITCH   Start by making a straight stitch from A to B. Make a second straight stitch from C to D. If you're making a row of cross stitches, you can first make a row of the underlying stitches (A to B) and then go back and cross them all at once.

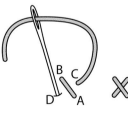

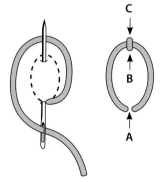

LAZY DAISY   Bring your needle through the fabric at A and put it back down in the same spot, but don't pull the floss all the way through; leave a small loop. Now bring your needle back through the fabric inside the loop at B and back down at C, catching the loop at the top and securing it to the fabric. Repeat this stitch in a circle to make a daisy.

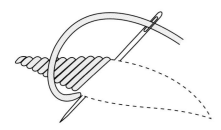

SATIN STITCH   The satin stitch is composed of parallel rows of straight stitches and is often used to fill in an outline.

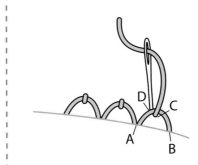

SCALLOP STITCH   Scallop stitches are great for making flowers or leaves, or stitch several in a row to make a pretty border. Make a loose stitch from A to B and press it flat to one side with your finger. Bring the needle to the front of the fabric at C, inside the loop. Insert the needle at the outside of the stitch, at D, to hold it in place.

SPLIT STITCH   This stitch is similar to the stem stitch, but as you bring the needle backward along the line, you poke it back through the previous stitch, splitting the strands of floss.

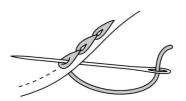

STEM STITCH   The stem stitch is perfect for stitching curved lines or flower stems, which is how it got its name. Make a stitch from A to B, leaving the floss a little loose. Pull the needle to the front again at C, between A and B and just to one side. Pull the floss tight and continue to form a line of stitches.

STAR STITCH   Make the Star Stitch the same way as the Cross Stitch, but add an addition stitch on top of it, from A to B. For the circle method, make several Straight Stitches in a circle, ending at the same center point. Make your first stitch from A to B, your second stitch from C to B, and so on around the center adding as many stitches as you like until you reach the first stitch.

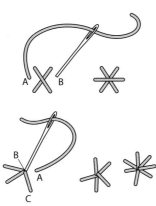

STRAIGHT (OR RUNNING) STITCH   Make this stitch by weaving the needle through the fabric at evenly spaced intervals.

STAB STITCH The stab stitch is a variation of the straight stitch using very tiny stitches. It's most often used to attach one piece of felt to another. To make almost invisible stab stitches, use thread or floss in a color to match the felt and make sure the stitches on the back of the felt are longer than the tiny stitches on the front.

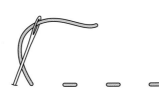

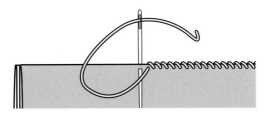

WHIPSTITCH   Also called the overcast stitch, the whipstitch is used to bind edges to prevent raveling or for decorative purposes. Simply stitch over the edge of the fabric.

ornaments

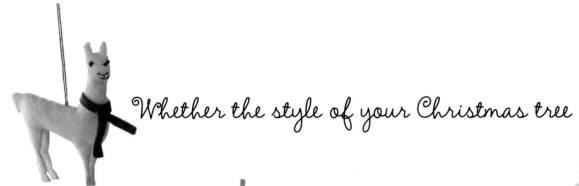

Whether the style of your Christmas tree

is muted and natural,  sparkly and bright, or leans

toward mod, all it takes is felt plus a stitch or two

(or perhaps a dab of glue) to make perfect ornaments

 aplenty. Create some for yourself and some to give

away as gifts. Everyone loves handmade!

But for the quick stitches
to make his mod argyle,
this foxy fellow is a
no-sew project.

Argyle Fox

DESIGNER: JENNIFER JESSEE

WHAT YOU NEED

Basic sewing kit (page 7)

Templates (page 116)

Gray felt, 9 x 12-inch (22.9 x 30.5 cm) sheet

Felt scraps in orange, cream, brown, green, and light blue

Blue thread

8 inches (20.3 cm) of ribbon

WHAT YOU DO

1 Using the templates, cut two gray circles, one orange fox body, one cream fox face, one brown nose and two brown eyes, two green diamonds, and one blue diamond.

2 Using the photo as a guide, glue the face onto the fox. Glue the eyes and nose in place on the face.

3 Place all three diamonds on the fox's belly, and glue them in place.

4 Wait for all the glue to completely dry. Machine-stitch a tall, narrow X shape over each diamond to create an argyle sweater effect.

5 Glue the finished fox figure onto one of the gray circles, being careful to keep it centered.

6 Cut an 8-inch (20.3 cm) piece of ribbon and fold it in half. Using the second gray circle for the back, sandwich the ribbon between the front and back circles, leaving a 2½-inch (6.4 cm) loop sticking out on top for the hanger.

7 Glue the circles together with the ribbon between them, being careful to keep the circles aligned.

Ornaments

These colorful felt and fabric
baubles have a sparkly seed-bead
edging. Mix and match your chosen
colors across the set.

Beaded Star Baubles

DESIGNER: LAURA HOWARD

WHAT YOU NEED

(to make the set of four baubles)

Basic sewing kit (page 7)

Templates (page 116)

Felt in four bright colors, approximately 3 x 6 inches (8 x 15.2 cm) of each color

Matching narrow ribbons, approximately 7 inches (17.8 cm) of each color

Matching embroidery floss

Quilting cotton or other patterned fabric in two bright colors, approximately 2½ x 4½ inches (6.4 x 11.4 cm) of each color

Sewing threads to match all the felt and fabric colors

Seed beads to match the fabric colors

Polyester stuffing

Iron-on interfacing (optional)

WHAT YOU DO

To make one bauble

1 Use the templates to cut out two felt circles. Trace the star template onto a piece of tracing paper and cut it out. Use the tracing paper template to cut out one fabric star; the transparent template will allow you to position the star just where you want it on the fabric print.

TIP: The fabric star may fray slightly. To prevent this, use iron-on fusible interfacing (following the manufacturer's instructions) or use printed felt instead of fabric.

2 Pin the star in the center of one of the felt circles, and sew it in place with small whipstitches in matching thread.

3 Decorate the space around the star with embroidery floss in a third color. Using three strands of floss, sew five stitches on each side of the star, using the photo as a guide.

4 Cut a 7-inch (17.8 cm) piece of narrow ribbon to match the felt circle and fold it into a loop. Using matching sewing thread and the whipstitch, sew it to the top of the undecorated circle so the cut ends overlap the felt slightly. Attach the loop by sewing into the felt, but not through it.

5 Place the two circles together so the ribbon ends are sandwiched between them. Using three strands of floss to match the decorative stitching in step 3, begin sewing the edges of the circles together with blanket stitch, keeping your stitches as even as possible and adding one seed bead to your thread before you sew each stitch, so the beads are sewn to the edge of the circle.

6 Sew most of the way around the bauble, leaving a small gap unstitched. Stuff the bauble lightly, then close up the gap with more beaded blanket stitches. Finish your stitching neatly at the back.

Pressing cloves into oranges is a sweet-smelling tradition that goes back hundreds of years. This stitched version makes a great gift and is filled with the scent of cloves!

Clove-Filled Orange Pomander Ornaments

DESIGNER: MOLLIE JOHANSON

WHAT YOU NEED

(to make one ornament)

Basic sewing kit (page 7)

Templates (page 116)

Orange felt, 3 x 6 inches (7.6 x 15.2 cm)

Brown embroidery floss

Whole cloves, 1 heaping tablespoon

Ribbon, 10 inches (25.4 cm)

WHAT YOU DO

1 Choose one of the orange pomander designs and trace it onto tracing paper. Use this as a template to cut two circles from the orange felt, then pin the tissue paper to one of the circles.

2 Stitch through the paper and felt at the same time to add the embroidered cloves and face. Using three strands of floss, embroider the cloves and eyes with French knots, and embroider the mouth with the scallop stitch. Carefully tear away the paper.

TIP: If you want to stitch both sides of the orange, simply omit the face on the back.

3 Place the embroidered circle on top of the plain circle and stitch around the edge using three strands of floss and the straight stitch. Leave an opening and fill the orange with whole cloves. Stitch the opening closed.

4 Cut a 3½-inch (8.9 cm) piece of ribbon and form it into a loop. Stitch the ends together with a few stitches. Use the remaining ribbon to tie a small bow. Stitch the ribbon loop and bow to the top of the orange, making sure that you catch all of the layers and that your stitches only go through the back of the bow.

Ornaments

Add a touch of Swedish charm to your holidays with a felt Dala horse ornament.

Dala Horse Ornament

DESIGNER: KATHY SHELDON

WHAT YOU NEED

Basic sewing kit (page 7)

Templates (page 118)

Red felt, 9 x 12-inch (22.9 x 30.5 cm) sheet

Felt scraps in turquoise and gold

White, turquoise, red, and gold embroidery floss

WHAT YOU DO

1 Use the templates to cut two Dala horse shapes from the red felt; the mane and the large saddle shape from the turquoise felt; and the small saddle shape from the gold felt. Make the little cuts to the mane shown on the template.

2 Transfer the embroidery lines onto the front of one horse piece.

3 Place the turquoise saddle on the horse's front and use four strands of the white floss and the straight stitch to attach it in place, leaving the top of the saddle unstitched.

4 Place the gold saddle on top of the turquoise saddle and use four strands of the white floss and the straight stitch to attach it in place, again leaving the top of the saddle unstitched.

5 Place the turquoise mane onto the horse, using the photo for placement. Use turquoise thread and small, closely spaced vertical straight stitches to attach the mane to the horse front. Leave the top of the mane unstitched.

6 Use six strands of the white floss and the split stitch to embroider the bridle. Use the six strands of the white floss and two closely spaced lines of the split stitch to embroider the chest and stomach straps.

7 Align the front and back horse pieces, embroidered side up. To begin attaching the front and back together, start at the left top of the saddle and use three strands of the red floss and the straight stitch around the outer edge of the horse. When you get to the mane, take care to pierce the back of the turquoise felt only without bringing the needle through to the front, then continue stitching through both layers of the red felt around the horse until you reach the other side of the saddle. Tie off at the back of or inside the horse.

8 Use two strands of the gold floss and the straight stitch to continue attaching the front and back pieces, this time going all the way through the red (two layers), turquoise, and gold felt with each stitch.

9 Cut about a 7-inch (17.8 cm) length of the turquoise embroidery floss and thread it onto a needle. Poke the needle through the top of the Dala horse's neck to find the point where the horse balances, then pull the floss through and tie it off to form a loop to hang the horse.

These delicate doves would love
to perch peacefully on your tree.

Dove Ornaments

DESIGNER: CHRISTI WHITELEY

WHAT YOU NEED

Basic sewing kit (page 7)

Templates (page 118)

Cream felt

Silver metallic embroidery floss

Silver metallic thread

Silver beads

Lavender embroidery floss

Polyester stuffing

Scallop fabric shears

WHAT YOU DO

1 Pin the templates onto two layers of felt. Using the scallop shears, cut around the outer edge of the each template, making sure each scallop cut is completed as you go around.

2 Using a single strand of silver embroidery floss and the photo as a guide, sew a backstitch all the way around the front (or top) layer of one left and right wing. Then stitch the center flourish with a lazy daisy stitch and a few straight stitches.

3 Pin the wing backs and fronts together, lining up the scallops.

4 Using the silver thread and working between each scallop, blanket stitch the front and back wing shapes together.

5 Use the silver thread to stitch the beads to either side of the bird's head for eyes.

6 Using two strands of lavender floss, stitch through the center of the lazy daisy to tack the wings into position on each side of the bird body.

7 Pin the bird body sides together, carefully lining up the scallops. Using a single strand of lavender floss and a single strand of silver floss together, blanket stitch around the entire bird body, working between the scallops and leaving an opening at the bottom for stuffing (don't cut or tie off the floss).

8 To make the hanger: thread three strands of silver embroidery floss onto a needle, knot the floss end, and poke the needle and floss through the inside top of the head and then down through the outside top of the bird at mid back. Tie off with a knot on the inside of the bird.

9 Stuff the bird body, and then blanket stitch the opening closed.

Once the luscious lashes of this Christmas llama seduce you, you'll want to stitch up a whole herd.

Fa la la la la Llama

DESIGNER: KATHY SHELDON

WHAT YOU NEED

Basic sewing kit (page 7)

Template (page 118)

Tan felt, 9 x 12-inch (22.9 x 30.5 cm) sheet

Maroon felt scrap

Black, light tan, medium tan, and turquoise embroidery floss

Stuffing

Bamboo skewer, toothpick, or other tool to poke stuffing into corners

WHAT YOU DO

1 Using the template, cut two llama shapes from the tan felt, making sure to cut along the black, outer lines only.

2 Transfer the embroidery designs for the face and the legs onto the front llama piece. (The lines delineating the legs, toes, and chin aren't stitched until step 6.)

3 Use three strands of the black floss to embroider the llama's face. The mouth and nose are made with the backstich and small French knots for the nostrils. To make each eye, make three straight stitches to form a triangle, then knot the floss on the back of the felt, but don't cut the floss. Instead, pull the remaining floss back through to the front of the felt at the upper right side of the triangle. Now cut the floss, leaving enough to form long eyelashes.

4 Align the embroidered front piece, right side up, on top of the back piece. Starting at the center of the llama's back and working toward its rump, use one strand of light tan floss and the blanket stitch to stitch the front and back of the llama together. Stitch all the way around, ignoring the leg and toes lines, and stopping when you have about a 1½-inch (3.8 cm) opening at the top of the llama's back, but don't tie off or cut the floss.

5 Gently add the stuffing to the inside of the llama, using the skewer or small tool to carefully poke the stuffing into the legs, head, and ears—don't overstuff. Then finish blanket stitching the front and back together, knotting the floss in the back.

6 Starting and ending on the back side of the llama, use the medium tan floss and the backstitch to embroider the llama's legs, toes, and chin lines. You'll be stitching right through the back, the stuffing, and the front with each stitch. For the chin line, go through the stuffing, but just barely grab the back felt with each stitch. Knot the floss at the back of the llama.

7 Cut a small strip of the maroon felt to make the llama's scarf. Tie the scarf around the llama's neck and make one small hidden stitch at the back where the scarf overlaps to tack down the scarf (it won't show, so you can use whatever color floss is in your needle).

8 Cut a 12-inch (30.5 cm) length of the turquoise embroidery floss and thread it onto a needle. Poke the needle through at the top of the llama's back to find the point where the llama balances, then pull the floss through and tie it off to form a loop to hang your llama.

Ornaments •

25

Make these ornaments as a set to hang on the tree or string them on baker's twine for a garland. This set would also look cute sewn from red or blue felt to make a Scandinavian-style winter village.

Gingerbread Village Ornaments

DESIGNER: LAURA HOWARD

WHAT YOU DO

To make each ornament

1 Cut out two matching building shapes from the ginger felt. Also cut out one of each of the snow pieces required from the white felt.

TIP: If you prefer, you can embroider the windows and doors first onto a piece of felt stretched in an embroidery hoop and then cut out the building shape. This will make it easier to embroider the design but will use up more felt.

2 Trace the building and its doors and windows onto a piece of white tissue paper. Cut around the building's outline and pin the paper onto a matching felt shape.

3 Use three strands of white floss to backstitch the doors and windows, taking care not to pull your stitches too tight and pucker the felt. Stitch as close as you can to the bottom of the doors, but don't worry about there being a small gap between your stitched line and the edge of the felt as you'll sew up the gap in a later step.

4 Remove the pins and carefully tear away the tissue paper to reveal the embroidered design.

5 Add the white felt snow shapes with white sewing thread. Sew each piece in place with a line of white running stitch along the inside edges only; the outside edge will be stitched in place when the whole ornament is sewn together later.

6 Cut a 7-inch (17.8 cm) length of baker's twine and thread a large needle with it. Take the undecorated backing piece of the ornament and sew one small horizontal stitch at the top so the ends of the twine are sticking out of the front side of the felt. Knot the loose ends of the twine together.

7 Place the front and back of the ornament together so the ends of the twine are sandwiched between them. Use three strands of white floss to blanket stitch the edges of the ornament together. Pull the twine loop out of the way as you sew past it. When you sew along the bottom of the doors, make sure you line up your blanket stitches so they fill in the gaps between the door and the edge of the felt. Leave a gap for stuffing.

8 Stuff the ornament, adding small pieces of stuffing at a time so the ornament doesn't get overstuffed. Sew up the gap with more blanket stitches and finish your stitching neatly at the back.

WHAT YOU NEED

(to make a set of four, one of each design)

Basic sewing kit (page 7)

Templates (page 120)

Ginger felt, two 9 x 9-inch (22.9 x 22.9 cm) squares

White felt, 4 x 5 inches (10.2 x 12.7 cm)

White embroidery floss

White sewing thread

Stuffing

Red and white baker's twine, 28 inches (71.1 cm)

TIP: Flip the house and cottage templates for some added variation in your village.

This cool cat will bring a retro vibe to your Christmas tree.

Kool Kristmas Kitty

DESIGNER: JENNIFER JESSEE

WHAT YOU NEED

Basic sewing kit (page 7)

Templates (page 123)

Pink felt, two 5 x 6-inch
(12.7 x 15.2 cm) pieces

Felt scraps in white, red, blue,
pink, green, and dark pink

Dark brown and red embroidery floss

Pink thread

Silver cord

WHAT YOU DO

1 To create the background, glue the two pieces of pink felt together. After the glue dries, cut the double layer down to a 3¾ x 4¾-inch (9.5 x 12 cm) rectangle. Trim the edges of the rectangle with pinking shears or scallop fabric shears.

2 Using the templates, cut a white oval and circle, green bow pieces, pink eye, blue eye, red nose, and two red ears.

3 Use six strands of dark brown floss and the satin stitch to create a pupil on each eye, and then glue each eye to the oval head.

4 Glue the red nose into place on the oval. Using six strands of red floss, make two single perpendicular stitches to create the mouth.

5 Using six strands of dark brown floss, make four single stitches to create whiskers.

6 Carefully glue the oval head onto the pink rectangle, referring to the photo for placement. Glue the red ears into place above, but closely touching the top of the head. Glue each piece of the bow into place, overlapping the head where needed.

7 Begin the body of the cat by machine-stitching one vertical and one horizontal line through the center of the white circle, crossing paths at center, with pink thread. Continue stitching straight lines through the center of the circle to create a star.

8 Glue the body onto the ornament just below, but touching, the oval head.

9 Cut a smaller rectangle that measures 3 x 3¾ inches (7.6 x 9.5 cm) from dark pink felt, then cut the edges with shears to match your pink rectangle base. Make a loop from an 8-inch (20.3 cm) piece of cord and stitch it to this smaller rectangle. Glue this smaller rectangle, with the stitched-on loop, to back of the ornament, being careful to keep it centered.

No Christmas tree is
complete without
a partridge and pears.

Partridge & Pears Ornaments

DESIGNER: LISA JORDAN

WHAT YOU NEED

Basic sewing kit (page 7)

Templates (page 123)

Stuffing

Jute twine

(for the partridge)

Various earth-tone shades and orange felted garment wool (see page 6) or wool felt

Earth-tones, orange, and black embroidery floss

Two black buttons (for eyes)

(for the pears)

Tan, green, gold, rust, plaid, and white felted garment wool (see page 6) or wool felt

White, black or brown, green, tan, gold, and rust embroidery floss

WHAT YOU DO

To make the partridge

1 Using the templates, cut two bodies, wings, faces, and belly shapes from the various earth-toned shades of felted fabric or felt. Cut two beak pieces from the orange felt.

2 Position the belly shape on the body, tacking it in place with a glue stick (or pins) and whipstitch into place using three strands of coordinating floss. Stitch only the top curve of the belly shape to attach it to the body. (The stitches on the outer edge of the shape will be done in the final steps.)

3 Position the face piece and beak and repeat the same steps. Position the wing shape on the body and whipstitch it into place, adding decorative stitches to suggest feathers. Repeat all the steps on the second body piece, making a mirror image.

4 Create a loop from the jute twine and place it at the top of the partridge's back, between the front and back pieces. Use the blanket stitch and three strands of the coordinating floss to sew the two pieces of the partridge together. Leave approximately 1 inch (2.5 cm) unsewn, and stuff the partridge lightly with the stuffing.

Continue stitching around the partridge, concealing the knot inside the stitches when finished.

5 Tie a knot in one end of three strands of black embroidery floss. Make a stitch where the button eye will go on one side of the partridge through to the other side. Stitch through the button, then back through to position the second button. Take a few stitches back through the two buttons until they are secure. Tie a knot and hide it.

To make the pears

1 Using the templates, cut two pear shapes from the tan, green, gold, or rust felt, one leaf shape from a contrasting shade of felt (see Tip), and one small interior pear shape from the white felt.

TIP: Use felted plaid garment wool as a playful variation for one leaf.

2 Position one white interior pear shape on top of one pear shape and whipstitch around the outside of the white piece with three strands of the white floss to attach.

3 Stitch down the center of the white interior pear shape to make two halves with a small oval in the center, where the seeds will go. Stitch two small pear seeds using the satin stitch and two strands of the black or brown floss.

4 Stitch the leaf vein down the center of one leaf. Weave the thread through the stitches on the underside of the leaf, and give a gentle tug to cause the leaf to curl slightly. Tie a knot on the underside of the leaf. Place the leaf shape at the top of the pear. Use three strands of matching floss to sew the leaf to the pear.

5 Create a loop from the jute twine and place it at the top of the pear, between the front and back pear pieces. Use the blanket stitch and three strands of the matching floss to sew the two pieces of the pear together. Leave approximately 1 inch (2.5 cm) unsewn, and stuff the pear lightly with the wool stuffing. Continue stitching around the pear, concealing the knot inside the stitches when finished.

Pink, Gold & Gray Ornament Trio

DESIGNER: JENNIFER JESSEE

Put on some Frank Sinatra Christmas tunes, pour a martini (hey, olives are red and green!), and craft yourself a merry mid-century Christmas.

Pink, Gold & Gray Ornament Trio

WHAT YOU NEED

(to make three ornaments)

Basic sewing kit (page 7)

Templates (page 124)

Light gray, pink, dark gray, gold, and white felt

Pink and dark gray embroidery floss

WHAT YOU DO

To make the bird ornament

1 Using the templates, cut two light gray background circles, one smaller pink circle, one dark gray bird with three tail feathers, one light gray wing, and one pink wing.

2 Cut a 9-inch (22.9 cm) piece of dark gray embroidery floss, and fold it in half. Glue the light gray circles together, sandwiching both ends of the floss between them to create a hanger at the top.

3 Glue the pink circle onto the gray background, being careful to keep it centered.

4 With six strands of pink floss, make two straight stitches through the center of each tail feather and a curved line for the bird's eye using the backstitch.

5 Glue the bird body and tail feathers onto the pink circle, using the photo as a guide for placement.

6 Glue the light gray feather onto the body and the pink feather on top of that.

To make the pink, gold, and gray bauble

1 Using the templates, cut two dark gray background circles, one smaller gold circle, one pink diamond shape, two pink triangle tips (you'll use these in step 6), and four dark gray teardrop shapes.

2 Cut a 9-inch (22.9 cm) piece of dark gray embroidery floss, and fold it in half. Glue the dark gray circles together, sandwiching both ends of the floss between them to create a hanger at the top.

3 With six strands of pink floss, whipstitch around the diamond shape, attaching it to the center of the smaller gold circle.

4 With six strands of pink floss, make three running stitches in each teardrop shape.

5 Glue the teardrop shapes to the pink diamond shape.

6 To make sure both points of the diamond shape are sturdy, glue the small triangle tips to the backside of the pink diamond after all the stitching around the edge is complete.

7 Glue the gold circle, with all the pieces attached, to the gray background.

To make the flower ornament

1 Using the templates, cut two gold background circles, one smaller dark gray circle, and all the other pieces needed for the flower. Use the photo as a guide as to which color each part needs to be.

2 Cut a 9-inch (22.9 cm) piece of dark gray embroidery floss, and fold it in half. Glue the gold circles together, sandwiching both ends of the floss between them to create a hanger at the top.

3 With the photo as your guide, glue all the flower pieces to the gray circle, starting with the large gold flower cup and the pink stem with leaves. Follow with the white flower cup, the gold flower cup, and then the pink dot.

4 With six strands of pink floss, make rows of straight stitches for the stamens onto the gray circle, just above the flower.

5 Glue the gray circle, with the finished flower attached, onto your gold background.

Ornaments

35

Hang this shining star
upon the highest bough!

Shining Star Tree Topper

DESIGNER: KATHY SHELDON

WHAT YOU NEED

Basic sewing kit (page 7)

Templates (page 127)

White felt, 9 x 12-inch (22.9 x 30.5 cm) sheet

Turquoise felt, two 9 x 12-inch (22.9 x 30.5 cm) sheets

Thin cardboard or cardstock, 7 x 6 inches (17.8 x 15.2 cm)

White and turquoise embroidery floss

Embroidery needle*

40 small iridescent blue-green crystal bicone beads

16 large iridescent blue-green crystal bicone beads

Two pieces green 22-gauge, covered floral stem wire, 18 inches (45.7 cm) long*

Hot sauce bottle or other cone-shaped object for shaping (see step 6)

Tape

WHAT YOU DO

1 Using the templates, cut one small star from the white felt and two large stars from the turquoise felt. Cut one small star from the cardboard (this goes inside for stability, so quick and slightly wonky will do here).

2 Trace the embroidery pattern onto the front of the white star.

3 Center the white star onto the front of one large turquoise star and pin it in place. Use two strands of white floss and the running stitch along the outside edge of the white star to attach it to the turquoise star, stopping at each star point to pick up a large bicone bead with the needle and add it to the point. Pull the thread tight and take an extra stitch to make sure each bead is securely attached to its point of the star.

4 Use two strands of the turquoise floss and the backstitch to begin embroidering the center vertical line of the interior star design, picking up a small bicone bead with the needle when you get to the third stitch. Continue adding a bead to the thread with every third stitch, making sure you end the center vertical line with two plain (beadless) stitches. Continue to use this method to embroider all the other lines, making sure you start and end each line with two plain stitches, pick up a bead with every third stitch, and skip over the bead at the center with all the rest of the lines.

5 Place the embroidered assemblage on top of the turquoise star back with the small cardboard star sandwiched in between. Starting at the small point on the bottom right side and stitching toward the top, use two strands of turquoise floss and the running stitch along the outside edges to begin attaching the two turquoise stars, stopping at every star point to pick up a large bicone bead with the needle and add it to the point. Pull the thread tight and take an extra stitch at each bead to make sure the bead is securely attached to its point of the star. Stop when you get to the small point on the bottom left, but don't cut or tie off the floss.

*****Note:** You'll need a needle with a hole that's large enough to accommodate two strands of floss but small enough to fit through the holes of the small beads. Look for floral stem wire in the artificial plants section of craft stores. You can substitute any wire you have on hand as long as it is strong enough to support the star but also bends easily.

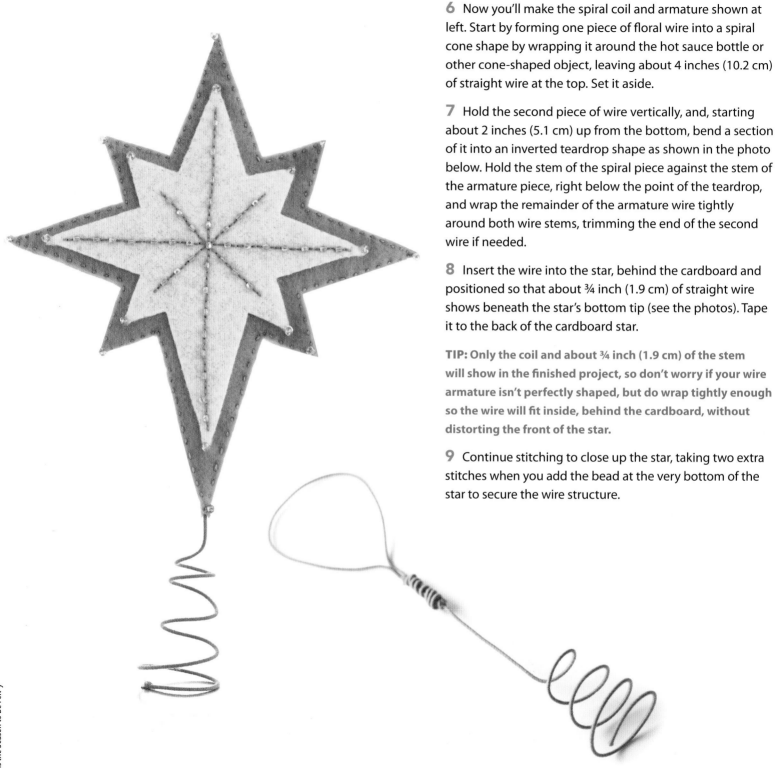

6 Now you'll make the spiral coil and armature shown at left. Start by forming one piece of floral wire into a spiral cone shape by wrapping it around the hot sauce bottle or other cone-shaped object, leaving about 4 inches (10.2 cm) of straight wire at the top. Set it aside.

7 Hold the second piece of wire vertically, and, starting about 2 inches (5.1 cm) up from the bottom, bend a section of it into an inverted teardrop shape as shown in the photo below. Hold the stem of the spiral piece against the stem of the armature piece, right below the point of the teardrop, and wrap the remainder of the armature wire tightly around both wire stems, trimming the end of the second wire if needed.

8 Insert the wire into the star, behind the cardboard and positioned so that about ¾ inch (1.9 cm) of straight wire shows beneath the star's bottom tip (see the photos). Tape it to the back of the cardboard star.

TIP: Only the coil and about ¾ inch (1.9 cm) of the stem will show in the finished project, so don't worry if your wire armature isn't perfectly shaped, but do wrap tightly enough so the wire will fit inside, behind the cardboard, without distorting the front of the star.

9 Continue stitching to close up the star, taking two extra stitches when you add the bead at the very bottom of the star to secure the wire structure.

Here's a quick, no-sew project
to add sparkle to your holidays.

Sparkly Icicles

DESIGNER: CHRISTI WHITELEY

WHAT YOU NEED

Basic sewing kit (page 7)

Template (page 128)

Iron-on adhesive

White stiff, glittery felt, two 8 x 10-inch (20.3 x 25.4 cm) pieces

Silver embroidery thread

Beads or sequins

WHAT YOU DO

1 Cut an 8 x 10-inch (20.3 x 25.4 cm) piece of the iron-on adhesive.

2 Sandwich the iron-on adhesive between the felt pieces, with the felt pieces glittery sides out. Press as directed on packaging.

3 Use the template as a rough guide to cut icicles out of the double felt layers. Use irregular, small rounded zigzags to cut down one side and then the other.

4 With needle and a single strand of the silver thread, puncture the icicle at the rounded end to create a hanger. Cut to desired length and secure with a knot.

5 Stitch or glue beads or sequins randomly for three-dimensional sparkle.

Layer up some candy-colored felt and create the sweetest treats to adorn your tree!

Sweet Treats Ornaments

DESIGNER: MOLLIE JOHANSON

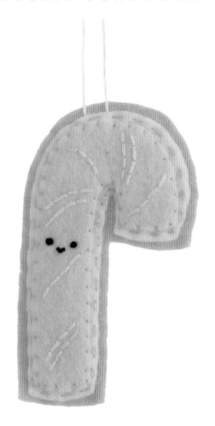

WHAT YOU NEED

(to make three ornaments)

Basic sewing kit (page 7)

Templates (page 128)

Felt scraps in pastels and coordinating darker shades

White felt, 4 x 5 inches (10.2 x 12.7 cm)

Black, white, and pastel embroidery floss

Tracing paper

WHAT YOU DO

1 Use the templates to cut out the three candy shapes from the pastel felt colors. Place the cut pieces onto white felt, then cut around each shape with about a ⅛ inch (3 mm) border to get a white shape that's slightly larger than the pastel shape. Place each white piece onto the coordinating darker felt, and cut around each shape with about a ⅛ inch (3 mm) border to get a dark shape that's slightly larger than the white shape. It's fine if the "hook" of the candy cane closes up.

2 Trace the embroidery details onto tracing paper, then lay them on each of the smallest candy shapes. Stitch through the felt and the paper using three strands of embroidery floss. Use white floss with the backstitch for the lines and French knots for the dots, and black floss with French knots for the eyes and a scallop stitch for the mouth. Carefully tear away the paper.

3 Layer the embroidered felt pieces onto the white pieces and stitch around the edge using coordinating floss and stab stitch. Layer the largest colored pieces behind and use coordinating floss and the straight stitch to stitch the layers together.

4 Thread a needle with three strands of white embroidery floss. Insert the needle between the two layers of felt at the top of each candy. Bring the needle back out, catching a couple of stitches to hold the thread in the layers of felt. Tie the ends of the floss together about 2½ inches (6.4 cm) from the ornament to form a hanger. Trim the ends.

Tea for three to hang
on your tree!

Teacup Ornaments

DESIGNER: KATHY SHELDON

WHAT YOU NEED

(to make three ornaments)

Basic sewing kit (page 7)

Templates (page 129)

Cream felt, 9 x 12-inch (22.9 x 30.5 cm) sheet

Felt scraps in blue, red, and gold

Cream, blue, red, and gold embroidery floss

Flower punch (optional)

Fabric glue (optional)

WHAT YOU DO

To make the blue and cream teacup

1 Use the templates to cut two teacup shapes from the cream felt, and four flower shapes, four leaf shapes, and three tiny circles from the blue felt.

TIP: Sometimes it's easier to just cut small details like the leaves and tiny circles free-hand rather than using templates—give it a try. Also, if you have the right size flower punch that can cut felt, you can use that for the flowers.

2 Transfer the embroidery pattern onto the front of one teacup shape (you can just draw little dots to indicate placement for the felt flowers, leaves, and three tiny circles).

3 To attach each felt flower to the teacup front, use two strands of the cream floss and the circle method for making a star stitch with a large French knot in the center. Use two strands of the blue floss and small French knot to attach each of the three tiny circles of blue felt at the top (interior) of the cup. Don't attach the felt leaves yet.

4 Use two strands of the blue floss to embroider the design on the cup's side and interior, but don't embroider the oval delineating the cup's opening yet. Stitch the tendrils coming out of the flowers and up

near the three felt circles using the backstitch and small French knots. Stitch the lines between the felt pieces with the backstitch. Use the satin stitch to attach the leaves.

5 Place the cup front, embellished side up, on top of the cup back piece, aligning carefully. Use three strands of the blue floss and the backstitch to embroider the oval delineating the cup's opening. Go through both pieces of felt as you stitch.

TIP: If you follow step 5, the back of the stitching for the opening oval will show on the ornament's back. If you will be hanging the cup where it will be visible from both sides, you can instead embroider the oval *before* you align the back of the cup with the front, but you will then need to use fabric glue to close the top of the ornament in step 6.

6 Starting at the upper left side of the cup, use three stands of the cream floss and the straight stitch to stitch down the left side of the cup, across the bottom, and up the outer edge of the handle to the right top of the cup to attach the front and back pieces together, tying off in the back. Use three strands of the cream floss to add a straight stitch around the inside of the handle. Repeat steps 2 through 6 with the red and gold felt and floss to make the matching teacups.

These wee teeter tots will
swing with holiday joy!

Teeter Tots

DESIGNER: SUZIE MILLIONS

WHAT YOU NEED

(to make three ornaments)

Basic sewing kit (page 7)

Templates (page 129)

White stiff felt, 9 x 12-inch (22.9 x 30.5 cm) sheet

Bone folder

Hot glue gun and glue sticks

2 foam balls, 1½ inches (3.8 cm)

Hobby saw or knife

Decorative ribbon, three 6-inch (15.2 cm) pieces

3 wood craft beads with a large hole

Black felt, 3 x 3 inches (7.6 x 7.6 cm)

Blue, red, and gold felt, 2½ x 2½ inches (6.4 x 6.4 cm)

Small scraps of brown, tan, and peach felt

Black fine-point marker & pencil

Toothpick

3 red seed beads

White pipe cleaner

Paper doily

Red thread

WHAT YOU DO

1 Trace the swing template three times onto the sheet of stiffened white felt, marking where to score. Cut out the shapes, and score with a bone folder.

2 Cut the foam balls in half with the hobby saw or knife. Put a small dab of hot glue in the center panel of each swing and glue a foam ball in place on each, flat side down, to form a snow hill.

TIP: When using hot glue on foam, put the glue on the object the foam is being glued to and let it sit for about 10 seconds so that the glue can cool slightly. The foam will shrink away a little less and make a better bond.

3 Glue the ends of the ribbon together to make a loop. Put the white felt swing on a flat surface and bring up the two side panels so they are centered over the bottom; sandwich the ribbon loop between the two narrow ends of the side panels and glue it in place. Let the glue on the loop cool and set, then slip the loop through the wooden bead, tug gently on the loop, and pull the bead down until the ends of the swing are tucked inside it. Repeat for the other two ornaments.

4 Cut six 1 x 1½-inch (2.5 x 3.8 cm) pieces from black felt to make the legs. One at a time, wrap each piece tightly around a toothpick and slide out the toothpick. Put a very fine line of hot glue down the open edge of the roll and hold until firmly sealed. Use the eraser end of a pencil to push two holes in the top of the white foam snow hill in each ornament. There should be about ⅛ inch (3 mm) of space between the holes; if they're too far apart, it will be hard to fit the parka over them; if they're too close together they're just not as cute. Put a dot of hot glue in each hole and press a roll of black felt into each, keeping the glued seams facing each other on the inseam.

5 Use the templates to cut out a parka and parka hood shape from the red, blue, and gold felt. Bring the two pointed ends of the parka together to form a cone. Put a narrow strip of hot glue under the overlap and glue in place. Put a dot of hot glue on the top of each leg and put the parka over the legs, pressing the back of the parka into the glue.

6 Cut out a face from the brown, tan, and peach felt. Stitch a red seed bead in the center of each face for the nose, then make two small eyes with a black fine-point marker. Put a small dot of glue a little below the center on the parka hoods and press the faces in place on each.

7 For each ornament, wrap the white pipe cleaner around the widest part of your thumb, hold that over the face and adjust so that the pipe cleaner hides the edge of the face. Cut the pipe cleaner and glue it in place.

8 Put a dab of hot glue on the top of each parka and press the heads in place, making sure they overlap the top of the parkas enough to fit neatly inside the frame of the swing.

9 To make the paper snowflake, cut out a round shape from a paper doily and use a very small dot of hot glue to attach it to the side of the swing.

decorations

Deck the halls  and everywhere else

in your home with these merry and bright decorations.

We've got garlands galore,  a poinsettia wreath

for your  door, and mistletoe to stand

beneath with the one  that you adore!

These felt decorations are sure to be

 treasured for years to come.

Have yourself a groovy
little Christmas with
this tweet bird mobile.

Bird Mobile

DESIGNER: JENNIFER JESSEE

WHAT YOU NEED

Basic sewing kit (page 7)

Templates (page 116)

Red and pink felt, 9 x 12-inch (22.9 x 30.5 cm) sheet each

Felt scraps in green and cream

Green, dark gray, and cream embroidery floss

6 green felt balls in various sizes (see page 9)

WHAT YOU DO

1 Using the templates, cut all the needed shapes, using the photo as a reference as to which shape is cut from which color. Cut two of each background shape.

2 With six strands of cream floss, use the backstitch to create a line down the middle of the green bird wing. Follow that with four straight stitches above and below the line to create a feather design.

3 With six strands of dark gray floss, stich the eye onto the head. Make one large loose stitch to create a curve followed by five short stitches to hold the curve in place and to serve as eyelashes.

4 Begin assembling the starburst pieces by gluing one of each pink circular shape onto the front of one red block, followed by a star shape on top. Set these two pieces aside to dry.

5 With the photo as a guide, assemble the bird block. Begin by gluing the largest red block on the largest pink block to create the background. Glue the bird body and head in place, leaving room for the tail feathers. Follow with the feathers and beak.

6 Hold the green floss double (so twelve strands total) and cut a 48-inch (122 cm) section. Thread the felt balls (see page 9) onto the floss with a large, sharp needle, carefully running the needle through the center of each ball, so the ball will hang evenly.

7 After all the balls are threaded, move them up and down the floss, leaving spaces for your felt blocks.

8 Place the finished bird block on top of the floss, centered between the middle two felt balls. Glue the front and back pieces of the block together, sandwiching the floss in between and down the middle.

9 Follow this same step with each of the starburst blocks, letting each dry before starting the next.

10 Tie a knot directly beneath the bottom felt ball, and trim off the tail. At the top, fold the floss over and tie a knot to create a loop, trimming the tail if needed.

This simple wreath mat makes a great
table decoration. Add a pine branch or two
in a jelly jar for cozy Christmas decor.

Christmas Is Coming Wreath Mat

DESIGNER: MOLLIE JOHANSON

WHAT YOU NEED

Basic sewing kit (page 7)

Templates (page 117)

Light green felt, ½ yard (.5 m)

White felt, ½ yard (.5 m)

Light blue felt, about 4½ x 11 inches (11.4 x 27.9 cm)

Green, white, and black embroidery floss

WHAT YOU DO

1 Using the template, trace four wreath pieces onto tracing paper. Cut them out and tape them together to form the large wreath shape. Use the template to cut out the wreath from green felt.

2 With the paper pinned onto the felt wreath, stitch each sprig of greenery. Using three strands of green floss, stitch along the sprig lines with the fern stitch. For visual interest, alter the size and direction of the stitch. After you've finished all of the embroidery, carefully tear away the paper.

TIP: Use your needle to perforate the paper as you go to remove it. Your needle will also be helpful to remove the small bits of paper that may get stuck under the stitches.

3 Cut out 24 berries from the white felt. Arrange them around the wreath, adding or removing berries as you like. Use fabric glue to attach the berries or stitch them in place.

4 Cut the bow pieces from the light blue felt. Embroider the face onto the bow wrap piece using three strands of black embroidery floss, and French knots for the eyes and a scallop stitch for the mouth. Fold the ends of the bow piece to the back so they overlap, and then stitch them together.

5 Wrap the bow wrap around the center of the bow, and stitch the ends together. Attach the bow to the wreath with fabric glue or stitch it in place.

6 Pin the green wreath onto the white felt and stitch around the outside and center openings with three strands of white embroidery floss and the straight stitch. Trim the outer edge of the white felt with scallop or pinking shears, leaving about ¼ inch (6 mm) of white showing. Leave the center of the wreath mat solid.

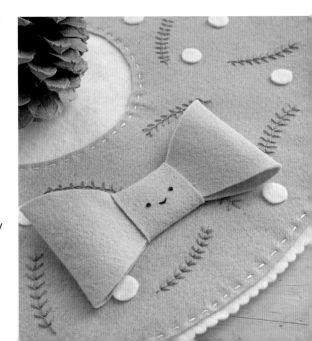

These star ornaments
will look great dangling from hooks,
doorknobs, or anywhere else you hang them!

Dangling Star Ornaments

DESIGNER: LAURA HOWARD

WHAT YOU NEED

(to make five ornaments)

Basic sewing kit (page 7)

Templates (page 118)

Felt scraps in assorted colors, between 2 x 2½ inches (5 x 6.4 cm) and 7½ x 7½ inches (19 x 19 cm) of each color

Matching embroidery floss

Matching sewing threads

Felt balls (see page 9)

WHAT YOU DO

To make each ornament

1 Use the templates provided to cut out the five pieces that make up the large star. Cut each piece from a different color or use a mix of three colors as pictured.

2 Choose another felt color to use as the backing for the large star. Sew the five pieces onto this backing felt (in number order) with whipstitch and matching sewing threads.

3 Cut around the star shape leaving a narrow border of the backing felt. Use this large star shape as a template to cut out two more large stars from matching felt.

4 Choose two of the colors you used for the large star pieces in step 1. Use the small star template to cut out three stars from each of these felt colors.

5 Cut a long piece of coordinating embroidery floss, and tie a large knot at one end. Thread a large, sharp needle with the floss and sew it through a coordinating felt ball (see page 9), carefully running the needle through the center of the ball, so the ball will hang evenly. Pull the thread through the ball until the ball reaches the knot then trim any excess thread below the knot.

6 Use long running stitches to sew three plain felt stars (two small stars and then one large star on top) onto the embroidery floss, so you now have three stars (each a different color) and a felt ball dangling on the floss. Leave a small gap between each shape and create a loop at the top by sewing the floss back into the large star and securing it with a knot or a few small stitches.

7 Place three matching stars together so that the star that has been stitched onto the floss is sandwiched in the middle of the other two matching stars (or, in the case of the large star, the pieced front star and the plain backing star shapes). Hold the layers together and sew their edges together with whipstitch and matching sewing thread. Repeat this step to sew the other two stars.

TIP: If you're making a set of these ornaments, make sure the floss loops and the spaces between the shapes are roughly the same size for each ornament.

Bring some evergreen charm into your holiday décor with a string of simple trees. Decorate your trees with stitched holiday ornaments or leave them plain for graphic impact.

Easy Tree Garland

DESIGNER: AMANDA CARESTIO

WHAT YOU NEED

(to make five ornaments)

Basic sewing kit (page 7)

Template (page 118)

Scraps of green felt in five shades, each at least 5 x 6 inches (12.7 x 15.2 cm)

Matching thread

Stuffing

Scraps of brown and tan felt, 1 x 3 inches (2.5 x 7.6 cm) each

Brown yarn (for hanging)

WHAT YOU DO

1 To create one tree, use the template to cut a tree shape from one end of a green felt scrap.

2 Pin the cut shape to the uncut end of the green felt scrap. Stitch around the side edges, leaving the bottom straight edge unstitched.

3 Cut the tree out from the bottom layer, using the top piece as a guide.

4 Stuff the tree slightly.

5 Fold a tan or brown scrap in half and insert the raw ends between the bottom straight edges of the tree shapes.

6 Stitch across the bottom straight edge of the tree, securing the trunk and the stuffing inside.

7 Use pinking shears to cut through the loop in the trunk shape.

8 Repeat steps 1 through 7 for the other four trees.

9 Leaving about 18 inches (45.7 cm) on either end (to hang the garland), hand-sew the trees to the yarn with a few simple stitches, placing them about 5 inches (12.7 cm) apart.

All is merry
and bright
with these
cheerful
patchwork
trees.

Felt & Fabric Trees

DESIGNER: CYNTHIA SHAFFER

WHAT YOU NEED

(to make the shortest tree)

Basic sewing kit (page 7)

Templates (page 119)

Teal green felt, 9 x 12-inch (22.9 x 30.5 cm) sheet

Gray felt, two 9 x 12-inch (22.9 x 30.5 cm) sheets

Two 12 x 12-inch (30.5 x 30.5 cm) teal cotton prints

Lightweight cotton batting, 12 x 12 inches (30.5 x 30.5 cm) square

Gray sewing thread

Black perle cotton or black embroidery floss

Two foam cones, 2⁷/₈ x 5⁷/₈ inches (7.3 x 14.9 cm)

Permanent spray adhesive

Temporary spray adhesive

Stuffing

Toothpick (Optional)

Craft glue

WHAT YOU DO

1 Trace or copy template A onto paper and cut it out. In steps 2 through 9 you'll be sewing together strips of felt and fabric to make a pyramid-shaped pieced panel of felt and printed fabric. You'll then use the template to cut the correct shape from the pieced panel, so as you add the strips of felt and fabric, use the template to check that your pieced panel is large enough.

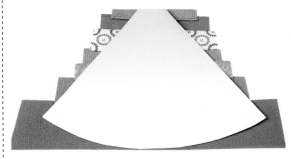

2 Working from the bottom up, cut a rectangle from the teal felt that measures 12 x 3 inches (30.5 x 7.6 cm). Cut a rectangle from the gray felt that measures 9 x 2 inches (22.9 x 5.1 cm).

3 Overlap the teal felt on top of the gray felt by ¼ inch (6 mm), centering them. Sew the two pieces of felt together.

4 Cut a rectangle from one of the cotton prints that measures 7½ x 1½ inches (19 x 3.8 cm). Center the print rectangle on top of the gray felt with right sides facing and the top edges aligned. Stitch the pieces together along the top edge with a ¼-inch (6 mm) seam allowance. Press the cotton strip up. You should now have a three-tier pyramid with the teal felt on the bottom, then the gray felt, and then the teal print fabric.

5 Cut a gray felt rectangle that measures 7 x 1¼ inches (17.8 x 3.2 cm). Follow the method in step 4 to stitch it to the print rectangle, centered and with right sides facing. Press the felt strip up.

6 Cut a rectangle from the other print cotton that measures 6½ x 2¼ inches (16.5 x 5.7 cm). Stitch it to the gray rectangle, centered and with right sides facing. Press the cotton strip up.

Note: These materials and instructions are for the shortest teal tree. To make the medium tree, use a 3⁷/₈ x 8⁷/₈-inch (9.8 x 22.5 cm) foam cone with 1½ inches (3.8 cm) trimmed off the bottom. For the large tree, use a 3⁷/₈ x 8⁷/₈-inch (9.8 x 22.5 cm) foam cone. For both of these sizes, you'll need ¼ yard (22.8 m) of a darker shade of the colored felt and a 14 x 14-inch (35.6 x 35.6 cm) piece of batting.

7 Cut a rectangle from the teal felt that measures 6 x 1¼ inches (15.2 x 3.2 cm). Stitch it to the print rectangle, centered and with right sides facing. Press the felt strip up.

8 Cut a rectangle from the gray felt that measures 5 x 1 inches (12.7 x 2.5 cm). Stitch it to the top of the teal rectangle, centered and overlapping by ¼ inch (6 mm).

9 Press the pieced panel flat. Pin template A to the piece, and use it to cut the shape from the pieced panel.

10 Pin the cut panel on the batting, and use it to cut the same shape from the batting. Use the temporary spray adhesive to adhere the pieced panel to the batting.

11 Using the black perle cotton or embroidery floss, stitch decorative stitches along the seams.

12 Place the bottom of the foam cone onto a piece of teal felt and trace around the base with a pencil. Cut out a circle ³/₈ inch (9.5 mm) away from the traced line. Then cut out little wedges around the outer edge of the felt circle to just shy of the traced line.

13 Spray the teal circle with the permanent spray adhesive and adhere it to the bottom of the cone. Fold the cut edges up onto the sides of the cone.

14 Starting at the wide base and working your way up, wrap the pieced panel around the cone, using straight pins at the overlapping edge to hold the panel in place as you wrap it. The panel will overlap itself by about ½ inch (1.3 cm).

TIP: The batting may need to be trimmed back a bit at the over-lapping edge and at the very top of the tree.

15 When you get to near the top, stuff the tip of the cone, and then continue overlapping the pieced panel.

16 Use the black perle cotton or floss to whipstitch the pieced panel to the base with a slanted overcast stitch. Then stitch the overlap of the pieced panel closed with a whipstitch stitch, starting at the base and working your way up to the top.

17 To begin making the tree's base, first cut a slice of foam 1½ (3.8 cm) inches up from the bottom of the remaining foam cone. Set this piece aside (it can be used to make the base for the yellow

tree). Make a second slice 1½ (3.8 cm) inches up from the cone's new bottom. Place this second slice of foam onto a piece of gray felt, smaller end down, and trace around its circumference. Cut out the felt circle.

18 Cut a 3½-inch- (8.9 cm) wide strip of gray felt that's long enough to wrap around the base's edge with a slight overlap. Use spray adhesive to adhere the felt strip to the base, overlapping the ends and wrapping the edges over the top and bottom edges of the base. Use the spray adhesive to secure the felt circle to the smaller end of the base. This will be the bottom of the base—the top of the base is wider than the bottom and is not covered with felt.

19 Apply a generous amount of craft glue to the top of the foam base, center the tree onto the base, and set the assemblage aside to dry.

20 If you'd like to add a star, cut out two stars from the teal felt, using the star template D. Glue a toothpick in the center of one star. When the glue has dried, glue the second star on top of the first star, sandwiching the toothpick. Insert the toothpick into the top of the tree.

Set these tiny, twinkly felt houses on the mantel, and then wait patiently for Christmas fairies to slip inside.

Felt Light Up Village

DESIGNER: AIMEE RAY

WHAT YOU NEED

(to make four ornaments)

Basic sewing kit (page 7)

Templates (page 119)

Light green, green, aqua blue, red, and pink felt, 9 x12-inch (22.9 x 30.5 cm) sheet each*

Light green, green, aqua blue, red, and pink floss

Thread to match felt colors or 2 strands from matching floss (optional)

LED lights

*****Note:** Heavy wool or wool-blend felt works best with this project.

WHAT YOU DO

1 Use the templates to cut the felt house pieces. Cut two roof pieces, two sides, and one front and back for each house. Mix and match window shapes on the back wall and roof pieces as desired. Fold the doors open on the dotted line, then press with your fingernail or lightly iron the crease. Cut the holes indicated in the roof pieces.

2 For each house, start by sewing the side walls, front, and back together using the whipstitch and matching thread or two strands of matching embroidery floss. Stitch the front piece to a side wall, the back piece to the other side of the same wall, then the second side wall to the other side of the back piece. Leave the house flat while you decorate it with embroidery.

3 Add some embroidery to the house walls and roof pieces using your choice of colors and the stitches and patterns provided with the templates on page 119.

4 Now sew the two roof pieces together at the top (short) edge using the whipstitch and matching thread or two strands of matching embroidery floss. Then line up one edge of the roof with one top edge of the front or back wall and stitch it on using thread or floss matching the roof color. When you've stitched on the whole roof, finish the house by stitching the last two walls together.

5 Set your tiny houses over LED lights for a festive display.

Deck the halls (or any place
you please) with boughs
of felt holly!

Holly Leaf & Berry Garland

DESIGNER: CYNTHIA SHAFFER

WHAT YOU NEED

Basic sewing kit (page 7)

Templates (page 121)

Sage green, Christmas green, light olive green, dark olive green, and light apple green felt, 9 x 12-inch (22.9 x 30.5 cm) sheet each

Black perle cotton

Dime or other small circle to trace the berries

Red felt, 8 x 8 inches (20.3 x 20.3 cm)

WHAT YOU DO

1 Using template A, cut out the following leaves: one from the Christmas green, two from the sage green, one from the khaki green, one from the dark olive green, and one from the light apple green.

2 Using template B, cut out the following leaves: one from the sage green, one from the dark olive green, three from the light olive green, and two from the light apple green.

3 Pin one smaller leaf on top of each larger leaf, using whatever combinations of the greens you find pleasing. Use the black perle cotton to stitch each set of top and bottom leaves together with long straight stitches.

4 Using a dime or other small circle as a template, trace and cut out six holly berries from the red felt.

5 Cut a 50-inch (127 cm) length of black perle cotton, and use it to stitch the holly leaves and the berries together, starting with the top of the darkest leaf. Take a couple of stitches at the top tip of the leaf and then tie a knot. Pick up a holly berry and stitch through the berry, but do not knot the thread. Next, stitch through the next leaf, again taking several stitches through the tip, and then knot the thread. Continue in this manner until you have all the leaves and the berries on the perle cotton strand.

This felt hooped reindeer silhouette is the kindest way to hang some wildlife on your wall.

Hooped Reindeer

DESIGNER: CYNTHIA SHAFFER

WHAT YOU NEED

Basic sewing kit (page 7)

Templates (page 122)

5-inch (12.7 cm) embroidery hoop

Black spray paint

Cream and red felt, 9 x 12-inch (22.9 x 30.5 cm) sheet each

Lightweight fusible interfacing, 9-inch square (30.5 cm)

Craft knife and cutting mat

Black perle cotton

Cream perle cotton

12 inches (30.5 cm) black rayon ribbon

WHAT YOU DO

1 Spray the outer hoop black and set it aside to dry.

2 Center the inner hoop onto the cream felt, and trace around its outer edge with a disappearing or water-soluble fabric pen. Now mark a larger circle about 1 inch (2.5 cm) from the traced circle.

3 Cut out the larger felt circle, place it on the interfacing, and cut out a circle of interfacing. Fuse the interfacing to the backside of the felt.

4 Use the reindeer head template to cut out a circle of red felt.

5 Use a self-healing craft mat and craft knife to carefully cut out the reindeer head.

6 Center and pin the red felt circle onto the cream circle. Using the black perle cotton and the backstitch, stitch around the perimeter of the red felt circle, close to the outer edge.

7 Use the cream perle cotton and the backstitch to stitch around the outer perimeter of the reindeer head.

8 Center the cream felt circle on the inner hoop, then press the outer hoop onto the cream felt. You may need to adjust the screw

to accommodate the extra bulk from the felt and the interfacing.

9 Trim off any excess felt from the back, close to the hoop.

10 Loop the black ribbon through the screw and knot it at the ends.

This banner is so simple that, if you help cut out the letters (or purchase stick-on felt letters), kids can make it!

Joy to the World Garland

no sew

DESIGNER: KATHY SHELDON

WHAT YOU NEED

Basic sewing kit (page 7)

Templates (page 122)

White felt, 9 x 12-inch (22.9 x 30.5 cm) sheet
Red felt, 9 x 12-inch (22.9 x 30.5 cm) sheet
Turquoise felt, two 9 x 12-inch (22.9 x 30.5 cm) sheets
Lime green felt, two 9 x 12-inch (22.9 x 30.5 cm) sheets

Narrow lime green ribbon, 3 yards (2.7 m)

Freezer paper or printable freezer paper (see page 8)

Ink jet (not laser!) printer

Small, curved scissors

Scallop shears (optional)

Fabric glue

Note: Don't worry about cutting out all those letters and shapes: Freezer paper and small curved scissor make accurate cutting easier than you'd think.

WHAT YOU DO

1 Trace or print the letter templates onto freezer paper. Use printable freezer paper or cut a regular freezer paper to size and tape it wax-side-down to a regular sheet of printer paper and send that through your inkjet printer (see page 8).

TIP: For a different greeting on your banner, just type one up and use that as a template. Choose a simple font in bold in the largest size possible and space each letter apart by one or two spaces. You may need to print out your greeting and enlarge it to get the size desired. Count the letters and adjust the number of pieces needed for your custom garland

2 Iron the traced or printed freezer paper onto the sheet of white felt. Roughly cut around each letter, then use small, curved scissors to carefully cut out each letter. Remove the freezer paper from the felt.

3 Use the templates to cut 14 small red ovals, 14 large lime green ovals, and 14 extra large scalloped turquoise ovals from the felt. If you have scallop fabric shears, you can use those instead to cut the large turquoise ovals.

4 Use fabric glue to attach each letter to the center of one small red oval of felt and each lime green oval to the center of a scalloped turquoise oval. Set them aside to dry.

5 Use fabric glue to attach each red oval with a letter to the center of a lime green/turquoise assemblage. Set them aside to dry.

6 Once all the felt letter assemblages are dry, unravel the ribbon's full length across a long flat surface. Carefully place each felt piece on top of the ribbon, making sure to leave plenty of ribbon free on each end for hanging and to space the pieces a consistent distance apart (about ½ inch [1.3 cm] between letters and 2 inches [5.1 cm] between words). Double-check that you've got the letters in the correct order before the next step!

7 Use fabric glue to attach each letter assemblage to its place on top of the ribbon. You can eyeball this, but you want the bottom edge of the ribbon to be about 1 inch (2.5 cm) below the top of each scalloped turquoise oval. Press each piece along its entire length to make sure it's securely adhered to the ribbon.

8 Wait patiently for the garland to dry, and then hang it up and spread some joy.

Decorations

The gifts on this garland are
open on top so you can tuck
 tiny treats inside. Add numbers
to make an advent calendar
or use the pattern to make
individual ornaments.

Mini Gifts Garland

DESIGNER: LAURA HOWARD

WHAT YOU NEED

(to make a garland with four large and four small gifts)

Basic sewing kit (page 7)

Templates (page 123)

Four bright colors of felt, 9 x 12-inch (22.9 x 30.5 cm) sheet each

Matching sewing threads

Ribbon, ½ inch (1.3 cm) wide and 80 inches (203 cm) long

WHAT YOU DO

1 Use the templates to cut the following pieces for each gift you want to make, mixing and matching your chosen colors and using two colors (A and B) per gift. From felt color A, cut two gift shapes (large or small); from color B, cut one cross-shaped ribbon piece (large or small), bow, center circle, left ribbon, and right ribbon.

2 Pin the cross-shaped ribbon piece to one of the gift shapes. Use the straight stitch and matching sewing thread to sew the ribbon in place, sewing along all the inside edges of the ribbon and the top edge (the bottom and side edges will be sewn later).

3 Arrange the four pieces that make up the bow: the left and right ribbons, the bow, and the center circle. Hold the pieces in position in the middle of the gift and use the straight stitch and matching thread to sew around the circle, sewing all the layers in place.

4 Repeat steps 2 and 3 to make the rest of the gifts for your garland.

5 Cut a piece of ribbon, approximately 80 inches (203 cm) long. Trim the two ends of the ribbon at an angle to help prevent fraying.

6 Plan the arrangement of your garland so you get an even mix of colors. Pin the undecorated gift backs to the ribbon in the order you want, layering them so the ribbon is on top of the felt and ¼ inch (6 mm) below the top edge of each felt gift. Leave some spare ribbon at each end (for tying the garland) and a small gap between each gift, as pictured.

7 Sew the ribbon to each piece of felt using sewing thread to match the felt (color A). Sew two lines of running stitch along each section of ribbon where it joins the felt and remove the pins as you sew.

8 Place a gift front on top of a matching gift back and pin them together. Sew around the edge with small running stitches and matching sewing thread (color A), keeping the top edge open so the gift can be used as a pocket for small gifts. Repeat to sew all the gifts together.

Variations
Use the garland to create an advent calendar garland; simply make a strand of 24 or 25 gifts and stitch numbers onto the bow centers. Or use the templates and add a bit of stuffing between the front and back to create individual gift ornaments.

This large sprig of mistletoe will make a great addition to your festive décor—perfect for Christmas kisses!

Mistletoe Sprig

DESIGNER: LAURA HOWARD

WHAT YOU NEED

Basic sewing kit (page 7)

Templates (page 123)

**Sturdy dark green felt,
4½ x 5½ inches (11.4 x 14 cm)***

**Dark green felt, 5½ x 8 inches
(14 x 20.3 cm)**

2 pipe cleaners, 12 inches (30.5 cm) each

Dark green sewing thread

Narrow white ribbon, 7 inches (17.8 cm)

5 white felt balls (see page 9)

Glue gun and glue

*Note: 100 percent wool felt
works well for this project because
of its stiffness.

WHAT YOU DO

1 Use the leaf template to cut 10 leaves from the sturdy dark green felt. Flip half of these over so you have five pairs of right- and left-facing leaves.

2 Twist the two pipe cleaners together at their centers, then fold them in half and bend the ends to form your mistletoe branch shape, using the branch template as a guide.

3 Use the branch template to cut out two branch shapes from the dark green felt.

TIP: If you have trouble making your pipe cleaner branches fit the template, draw a template to fit your branches instead. Trace around the shape and then add a bit extra around the outside to create your own custom branch template.

4 Cut a 7-inch (17.8 cm) piece of narrow white ribbon, and fold it over to form a loop. Use dark green sewing thread and the whipstitch to sew the ribbon ends to the top of one of the felt branch shapes, sewing into the felt but not through it.

5 Sandwich the pipe cleaner branches between the two felt branch shapes, making sure the ribbon ends are hidden between

the layers. Hold felt branch shapes together and then, starting from the top, gradually whipstitch the edges of the felt branches together with matching thread so the pipe cleaners are sewn inside.

6 Use a glue gun to stick a pair of felt leaves to each of the branch ends, so the tops of the leaves overlap slightly. Glue the final pair of leaves higher up the branch, as pictured. Let the glue cool.

7 Add the felt balls (see page 9) as pictured, using the glue gun to stick one onto each pair of leaves where they overlap.

Here's a large, colorful poinsettia wreath that will stay fresh year after year.

Pretty in Pink Poinsettia Wreath

DESIGNER: SUZIE MILLIONS

WHAT YOU NEED

Basic sewing kit (page 7)

Templates (page 125)

3 light pink, 4 medium pink, 2 dark pink, 3 antique white, 1 light green, and 1 dark green felt sheets, each 9 x 12-inches (22.9 x 30.5 cm)

Green foam wreath, 14 inches (35.6 cm)

Plain pins

Ball head pins, white

Silver thread

Hot pink ribbon, 1 yard (1 m)

WHAT YOU DO

1 Cut the pink felt sheets into the following size rectangles:

- Large, 1¼ x 3 inches (3.2 x 7.6 cm): 36 light pink and 60 medium pink

- Medium, 1 x 2½ inches (2.5 x 6.4 cm): 12 light pink, 36 medium pink, and 12 dark pink

- Small, ¾ x 1½ inches (1.9 x 3.8 cm): 20 light pink, 60 medium pink, and 20 dark pink

TIP: You'll be cutting extra petals. Use the directions as a guide, but add an extra petal here and there as needed to cover the foam and make the wreath full.

2 Use the templates to cut each rectangle into a leaf shape at top. Cut out two at once to save time. The shapes can vary as you cut.

TIP: As you assemble each flower, use the medium pink as the base color and mix in the lighter and darker pinks spontaneously to make each flower unique.

3 Start one flower by attaching five large medium pink petals to the face of the foam ring to form the bottom layer of a bloom. To give each petal dimension, wrap both

edges of the wide base in toward the center and push a plain pin through all the layers as you attach.

4 Use the same method to attach two medium petals as the center layer. They can be in any position, next to each other, opposite one another, or any other combination of positions.

5 The top layer of the poinsettia consists of five small petals with the white ball head pins used instead of the plain pins to attach. Position the petals so that the white pins are somewhat evenly spaced as in the photos.

6 Add the next bloom to the ring, spacing it so it overlaps the last slightly, and then continue adding blooms all the way around the ring. There are 16 on the wreath shown.

7 To create the pom poms, cut the antique white felt into 2½-inch (6.4 cm) pieces, then cut the pieces into narrow strips, about ⅛ to ³⁄₁₆ inch (3 to 5 mm) wide. A rotary cutter is ideal for this job. Cut enough to make 12 piles of 20 strips.

8 Cut 36 strips of each of the other colors of felt. Add anywhere from one to three strips of the other colors to each pile of white strips. Add two to six pieces of silver thread to each pile.

9 Tie a piece of silver thread around the middle of each pile of felt strips and silver threads, pull it very tight, and then knot it. Trim the end of the silver thread to the same length as the felt strips. Fluff the pom pom to give it a ball shape. Trim any strips that are longer than the rest.

10 Pick a bloom to be top and center on your wreath. Tie a knot in the hot pink ribbon to make a 6-inch (15.2 cm) loop, and tie the loop to the top of the ring. Pin a cluster of five pom poms to a spot near the top of the wreath, facing out. Pin the remaining pom poms at even intervals on the inside of the ring.

11 Fluff and arrange the blooms.

Rustic Reindeer

DESIGNER: SUZIE MILLIONS

We dare you not to smile
as this reindeer comes together
in 12 steps and then perches
on your mantel.

Rustic Reindeer

WHAT YOU NEED

Basic sewing kit (page 7)

Templates (page 126)

Orange, coral red, and ivory felt, 9 x 12-inch (22.9 x 30.5 cm) sheet each

Brown felt scrap

Hole punch, 3/16 inch (5 mm)

Foam ball, 2 inches (5.1 cm)

Craft saw or steak knife

Hot glue gun and glue

2-inch (5.1 cm) diameter wood disc, 1/8 inch (3 mm) high

4 sticks for legs, 3 inches (7.6 cm) long*

2 clusters of twiggy branches for antlers *

Orange thread

Stuffing

Bamboo skewer

Pencil

WHAT YOU DO

1 Using the templates, cut out all the pattern pieces: cut the side and back panels from orange felt; the head, head strip, and ears from coral red felt; the belly, eyes, nose, and chest fur from ivory felt; and the rectangle for nostrils from dark brown felt. Use the hole punch to make the pupils from dark brown felt.

2 Cut the foam ball in half with the craft saw. Put a circle of hot glue on the wood disk and press one of the pieces of plastic foam ball into it to make the base. Put that aside for now.

3 With the flat surface down, cut about one-third from each side of the other half of the plastic foam ball, leaving a foam slice that is a little less than ¾ inch (1.9 cm) wide. With the arched surface facing up, press the four leg sticks into the flat bottom side. The back legs should be ¾ inch (1.9 cm) behind the front legs. One at a time, pull a leg out, put some hot glue in the hole and return the leg. Set aside.

4 To begin forming the tail, first match the rounded end of the felt back panel to the rounded end of the felt belly panel and pin the pieces together at that end. Starting 1 inch (2.5 cm) down from the end of the tail as marked on the template, whipstich the pieces together, 1/16 inch (1.6 mm) in from the edges. Stitch toward and then around the rounded end, continuing 1 inch (2.5 cm) down to the point opposite from where you started stitching.

5 Whipstitch the back panel to the side panels, but leave the head open where the two side panels meet.

6 Starting at the base of the tail, whipstitch the belly panel to one side panel, stopping just past the curve of the backside where a leg will go (marked on the template). Repeat with the other side panel.

7 Line the inside of the body with a thin layer of stuffing. Position the foam piece with the legs inside the body and add more stuffing around it to fill out the figure. Continue stitching to attach one side panel, stitching close to the legs and then passing the thread to the other side of the leg on the inside so there are no long stitches showing

*Note: Harvest your own sticks, or purchase them at a craft or floral store. The antlers and legs pictured are purchased birch sticks. Try to use sticks that are similar thickness with small knots that look like knees. Line the knees up then trim above and below to make the sticks 3 inches (7.6 cm) long.

on the outside. Add an extra stitch or two near the leg openings to keep them closed snugly. Stitch to the end of that side panel (at the tip of the nose), then knot and clip the thread. Starting at the base of the tail again, stitch the belly to the other side panel, ending again at the tip of the nose. Leave the face seam open until after you have stitched the head.

8 Trim the bottom edge of both head panels and both ends of the head strip with the pinking shears. Pin one ear in place on a head panel, pinching it a little at the base to make it dimensional. Stitch the head panel to the head strip. When you reach the ear, stitch it to the head panel along the seam and by catching some stitches on the interior surface of the felt without stitching through to the outside. Stitch the other head panel and ear in place.

9 Stuff a cotton-ball-size wad of stuffing into the head, enough to fill up the nose and cover the base of the ears. Stretch a hole on top of the head to put an antler through by pressing the pointed end of a bamboo skewer through the seam, just in front of the ear. Remove the skewer and carefully work the base of one of the antlers through the hole. Repeat for the other antler. Work the end of the glue gun into the stuffing on the inside edge of the antler and put a little glue there. Press the stuffing in toward the glue with the butt of the bamboo skewer. Avoid getting any glue on the felt, inside or out.

10 Glue the dark brown rectangle for the nostrils to the end of the nose. Glue the white patch over it, lining up the bottom of both pieces so they are even (use the project photos for reference). Glue the eyes in place.

11 Poke the legs into the foam base and press them down to get a stance you like. Before stitching the body closed, put the head on it to be sure there's enough stuffing in the neck to support it and to figure out where to place the patch of chest fur so that it hangs down below the head without the seam showing. Adjust the stuffing if needed; the body should be firm, but too much stuffing will stress the seams. Use the eraser-end of a pencil to press the stuffing further in and to direct any extra stuffing where it's needed.

12 Stitch the body closed. Trim the end of the patch of chest hair with pinking shears, and stitch it in place. Slip the head on the body. Fluff out the chest fur.

These chimes will help you ring in the holidays. Ding dong!

Ring My Bells Garland

DESIGNER: CHRISTI WHITELEY

WHAT YOU NEED

Basic sewing kit (page 7)

Templates (page 126)

Iron-on adhesive

Pink felt

Red felt

Red embroidery floss

Red/white baker's twine

WHAT YOU DO

1 Apply the iron-on adhesive to the pink felt, but don't remove the paper backing.

2 Cut out all the template pieces from red and pink felt, enough for five or six bells.

3 To begin making one bell, remove the paper backing from the pink clapper highlight piece. Position it on the red clapper piece, and iron to adhere it in place. With three strands of red floss, backstitch the pink highlight onto the clapper. Using three strands of red floss, whipstitch the red clapper front to the pink clapper back, working around the outside edge. Set aside.

4 Remove the paper backing from the other two pink highlight pieces. Position the highlights on the red bell shape using the project photo as a guide, and iron to adhere them in place. Using three strands of red floss, backstitch the highlights in place. Using three strands of red floss, backstitch the outline edge of the red bell shape.

5 Position the clapper behind the red bell front bottom rim, overlapping about ¼ inch (6 mm), and pin it in place. (Place the clapper in a different position for each bell so the bells will appear to be ringing.)

6 Remove the backing from two pink loop hangers, and iron to adhere them together.

7 Position the loop hanger behind red bell front top, overlapping ¼ inch (6 mm) and pin in place.

8 Remove the paper backing from pink bell back, and iron to adhere it behind the front bell, securing the clapper and hanger.

9 Cut six 8-inch (20.3 cm) lengths of baker's twine. Loop it onto the bell hanger and tie off with a knot—don't cut the twine.

10 Cut a 7-foot (2.1 m) length of baker's twine. Tie a loop at either end, and tie a knots along its length, one every 12 inches (30.5 cm). Tie each bell onto a knot, and tie the excess into a bow. Trim any excess twine.

This
cheerful small,
flat wreath is light
enough to hang
anywhere. Make it in
these subtle shades or
use more traditional
holiday colors.

Scrappy Wreath

DESIGNER: AMANDA CARESTIO

WHAT YOU NEED

Basic sewing kit (page 7)

Template (page 127)

Dark gray felt, at least 15 x 13 inches (38.1 x 33 cm)

Fusible webbing, at least 9 x 17 inches (22.9 x 43.2 cm)

Scraps of felt in three shades, at least 5 x 3 inches (12.7 x 7.6 cm) each

Scraps of fabric in five shades, at least 5 x 3 inches (12.7 x 7.6 cm) each

Two white metal eyelets, ¼ inch (6 mm), and a setter

Thin, lightweight rod, at least 10 inches long (25 cm) (A matchstick, straw, or chopstick will work!)

Yarn (for hanging)

WHAT YOU DO

1 Cut a 15 x 13-inch (38.1 x 33 cm) piece from dark gray felt. Pink the long side edges.

2 Cut three 3 x 17-inch (7.6 x 43.2 cm) strips from the fusible webbing. Trace the leaf template vertically along the strips. You'll need to trace about 33 leaves. Save any excess in case you need to cut more leaves later (as you lay out the wreath shape).

3 Cut the fusible web strips into sections, based on how many leaves you want to cut from each color of felt and fabric.

4 Fuse the cut sections to the back of the fabric and the felt pieces. Cut the shapes out and remove the fusible webbing's paper backing.

5 Place the leaves on the grey panel, using the project photo as a guide.

6 Iron the leaves in place, using a pressing cloth if needed. You may need to press a little longer over the felt leaves, but not too long!

7 Working your way around the wreath, stitch around the outer edge of each leaf.

8 Set the eyelets at the top of the wreath, 3½ inches (8.9 cm) from the outside edges and ¾ inch (1.9 cm) down from the top edge.

9 To make the rod casing, fold the bottom edge of the panel, about 1½ inches (3.8 cm), to the wrong side. Stitch ¾ inch (1.9 cm) in from the folded edge (or more if you're using a thicker rod) and insert the rod.

10 Cut a length of yarn and thread it through the eyelets, adding a bow if you like. All done!

These playful snow bunnies
will add charm to any
miniature Christmas tree.

Snow Bunnies Miniature Tree Skirt

DESIGNER: KATHY SHELDON

WHAT YOU NEED

Basic sewing kit (page 7)

Templates (page 128)

Light green felt, ½ yard (.5 m)

Cream felt, ½ yard (.5 m)

Tan felt, 9 x 12-inch (22.9 x 30.5 cm) sheet

White and dark brown felt scraps

Tan, white, dark brown, medium brown, dark green, light green, red, and cream embroidery floss

Large red rickrack

Temporary adhesive (optional)

WHAT YOU DO

1 Increase the templates for the skirt's small and large half-ring shapes as directed and trace the shapes onto freezer paper. Fold the light green felt in half, and iron the larger half circle onto it, placing the straight edges of the shape on the fold. Cut out the shape and unfold the felt to get a large ring shape. Repeat with the smaller half circle on the cream felt to get a smaller cream ring shape. Set the green ring aside.

2 Use the templates to cut out the five bunny outlines from the tan felt and five white bunny tails from the white felt. Use the templates to cut the three pinecones from the dark brown felt—cut the outlines first and then cut out the little notches on the sides. Set the bunnies and the tails aside for now.

3 Transfer the embroidery patterns for the pine boughs onto the front of the cream felt ring, using the photos for placement. Use the stem stitch to make the main branch of each bough. To make it appear tapered, start with six strands of the dark brown floss and then tie off and switch to four strands toward the end of the branch. To make the little twigs coming off each branch use four strands of

the dark brown floss and the stem stitch. Use three strands of dark green floss and light green floss and small single straight stitches to make the pine needles, and use six strands of medium brown floss to make the French knots for the tiny pine cones.

4 Using the photos as a guide, arrange the bunnies onto the cream ring of felt. Pin them in place. Use two strands of the tan floss and tiny straight stitches to attach the bunnies to the cream felt. Using small tight stitches here will give the bunnies a slightly raised appearance. Be sure to include the stitches that delineate the ears and legs.

5 To give each bunny a tail, first place the tail up against the bunny's rear, determine a pleasing tail shape for that bunny, and trim the felt carefully with small curved scissors if necessary. Use only one strand of the white floss and tiny stab stitches very close to the outside edge to attach each tail.

6 Use six strands of the dark brown floss to make a French knot for each bunny's eye. Add a tiny straight stitch to each French knot for detail (see Tip). Use four strands of dark brown floss and the satin stitch to give each bunny a nose.

TIP: To make expressive eyes, first make a French knot and then add a tiny straight stitch up close to the top of the French knot. Experiment a bit first on a scrap piece of felt to find the look you like because the placement and length of the stitch will change the bunny's expression.

7 Using the photos as a guide, place the felt pinecones on the cream felt. Use two strands of the medium brown floss and small straight stitches to attach the pinecones to the cream felt and add embellishment.

8 Place the cream felt on the green felt ring so that about ½ inch (1.3 cm) of green felt shows on the inside of the ring, and 1½ inches (3.8 cm) show on the outside edge of the ring. Pin the cream ring in place or adhere it to the green felt with spray adhesive.

9 Decide what you want the front of your tree skirt to be, and mark a straight line across the width of the ring (over both the green and cream felt), directly opposite the front (this will be the opening for the skirt at the back). Make sure this line doesn't interrupt any stitches or embellishments. Carefully cut on the line through both layers of felt.

10 Lift up the outer edge of the cream felt and, starting at the line you just marked in step 9, tuck the red rickrack underneath so that just enough of the rickrack peeks out to create a red scalloped trim all around the cream felt's edge. Trim the rickrack at each edge of the back opening. Attach the rickrack to the cream and the green felt using two strands of cream floss and small, widely spaced stab stitches, making sure you are going through all three layers (green felt, rickrack, and cream felt) with each stitch.

11 Use six strands of the red floss and the straight stitch to attach the cream felt to the green felt at the inner circle, starting and stopping at each edge of the back opening.

TIP: This miniature tree skirt should close itself sufficiently when covering a tree stand; if not, use the red or cream floss to loosely stitch up the opening once the skirt is in place, tying the ends of the floss in a bow that can be untied when it's time to remove the tree skirt.

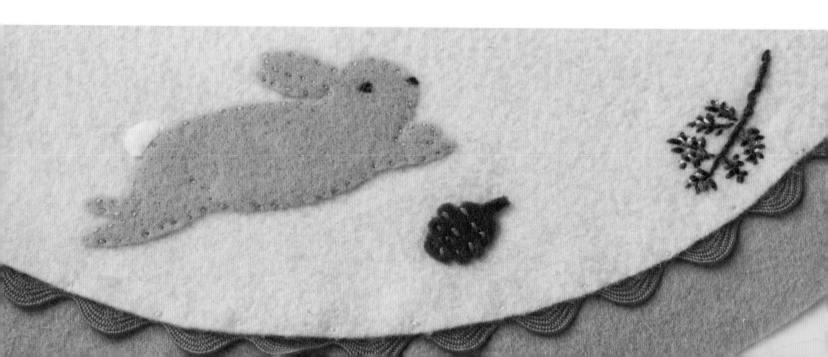

The tradition of the yule log
is thought to predate medieval
times—start your own
tradition with this adorable
felt version.

Yule Log

DESIGNER: AIMEE RAY

WHAT YOU NEED

Basic sewing kit (page 7)

Templates (page 129)

Light brown, brown, and green felt, one 9 x 12-inch (22.9 x 30.5 cm) sheet each

Felt scraps in light green, dark green, red, pink, and white

Green, brown, light brown, red, pink, and white embroidery floss

Stuffing

Three ½-inch (1.3 cm) red beads, or polymer clay and red paint, see Tip

TIP: You can easily make your own berry beads from polymer clay. Just make three ½-inch (1.3 cm) balls of the clay, and poke a hole through each with a needle. Make the holes off center, closer to one edge than the middle. Bake the beads according to the package instructions, and then paint them with red paint.

WHAT YOU DO

1 Cut out the templates, and pin them onto the felt. Cut out the felt pieces according to the template instructions: you'll need two or more of some pieces.

2 Start by transferring and then embroidering the designs onto the mushroom tops, leaves, and wood pieces according to the patterns on page 129.

3 To make the mushrooms, line up one color oval top and one white oval top and stitch them together around the edge using the straight stitch and one strand of the pink or red floss. Keep your stitches small and close together. Before closing it up, stuff a bit of stuffing inside. Fold the stem piece into a tube, overlapping the edges a bit. Stitch the ends together using one strand of white floss, and stitch the stem to the top piece using the whipstitch. Repeat for the second mushroom.

4 To make the stump branch, fold the base piece into a tube, overlap the edges ¼ inch (6 mm), and sew them together using one or two strands of the dark brown floss. Now stitch the end piece over the flat end (the curved end will attach to the log) using the whipstitch and the brown floss. Stuff some stuffing inside and set it aside.

5 Fold the log piece into a tube with the seam at the bottom; pin the seam. Arrange the branch, leaves, and mushrooms onto the top of the log piece, using the photo as a guide). Remove the pins from the log seam, lay the log piece flat, and begin stitching everything in place using the whipstitch and one strand of matching embroidery floss. Fold the pine needles in half once or twice before stitching them on.

6 Sew the berries onto the log over the felt leaves.

7 Fold the log piece into a tube, overlapping the edges ½ inch (1.3 mm), and sew the edges together with brown floss. Position one end piece over the hole on one end and sew it in place using the whipstitch. Stuff the log with stuffing, and then sew on the other end piece.

stockings & more

 Santa has seen a lot of stockings

in his day, but even he'll be impressed

with our collection,  from one with its own

 wee pocket gnome to an elegant  one scattered

with colorful stars. And we couldn't

stop at stockings, so we squeezed in a few bonus

 projects—just because we

fa la la la felt like it!

Felt is available in an awesome
rainbow of colors and this
project really shows them
off! Don't fancy making
a rainbow stocking?
Just mix and match
your favorite
colors instead.

Rainbow Star Stocking

DESIGNER: LAURA HOWARD

WHAT YOU NEED

Basic sewing kit (page 7)

Templates (page 126)

White felt (100% wool or other sturdy felt), 17 x 22 inches (43.2 x 55.9 cm)

Felt in 32 assorted colors,* up to 4 x 4 inches (10.2 x 10.2 cm) of each color

Matching sewing threads

Matching embroidery floss

White ribbon, ¾ inch (1.9 cm) wide and 8 inches (20.3 cm) long

*Note: You've got lots of options when it comes to colors. For a subtler look, try using only one or two colors in a variety of shades.

WHAT YOU DO

1 Use the template provided to cut out two white stockings.

2 Before cutting the stars, arrange the 32 colors of felt so they transition from reds and yellows to pinks and purples and then to blues and greens. For each star, use the templates to cut out two star shapes, A (bottom layer) and B (top layer) made up of two shades of felt that are next to each other on the spectrum. Use the photo as a guide to arrange the stars on the stocking front as you cut, and change the colors of the stars as you move down the stocking

3 Take a digital photo or make a quick color sketch, then remove the top layer of stars. Pin the bottom layer of stars in place, leaving room around the edge of the stocking for blanket stitching to be added later.

4 Use matching sewing thread to sew each star in place with a line of small straight stitches around the edge.

5 To add the next layer of stars, pin or hold each smaller star in place in the middle of its "matching" larger star. Use three strands of matching floss to sew five lines of neat straight stitches out from the center of the

small star to a point, sewing the final stitch in each line over the small star's point to hold it in place. Then sew back toward the center with more straight stitches to create a continuous line of stitching. Repeat this until all the stars have been sewn in place.

6 Cut an 8-inch (20.3 cm) piece of white ribbon. Fold the ribbon to form a loop. Place it in the top right corner of the back stocking piece, a little in from the edge so the ribbon ends overlap the stocking top by about 1 inch (2.5 cm). Whipstitch the ribbon in place with white sewing thread, sewing into the felt but not through it.

7 Cut a 1 x 1½-inch (2.5 x 3.8 cm) piece of white felt and place it over the ribbon ends. Attach it with small straight stitches and white sewing thread, sewing around the rectangle and then across it in an X shape so the felt and ribbon are securely sewn in place.

8 Pin the front and back of the stocking together and trim any excess felt from the edge of the back stocking shape. Blanket stitch the edges of the stocking together with matching white sewing thread, leaving the top of the stocking open.

Santa Gnome is coming to town! And he's got his own little stocking pocket to peek out from on Christmas morning.

Santa Gnome Stocking

DESIGNER: AIMEE RAY

WHAT YOU NEED

Basic sewing kit (page 7)

Templates (page 127)

Light green, green, aqua blue, and red felt, 9 x12-inch (22.9 x 30.5 cm) sheet each

Scraps of white and peach felt

Light green, aqua blue, red, white, and dark brown embroidery floss

Stuffing

WHAT YOU DO

1 Use the templates to cut out the following felt pieces. Cut two stocking shapes from the light green felt, one pocket from the green felt, one heel and toe and two body shapes from the aqua blue felt, one cuff and hanger strip and two hats from the red felt, one beard and hair (back piece) from the white felt, and one face from the peach felt.

2 Position the blue toe and heel, and the red cuff onto the front of one of the green stocking pieces and stitch them on using the straight stitch in a contrasting color of floss. Carefully trim away any of the green heel and toe behind the blue pieces if needed. Position the green pocket in the center and stitch it on around the bottom edge only, using the straight stitch and the green embroidery floss.

3 Pin the front and back stocking pieces together, and sew around the sides and bottom using the whipstitch and two strands of floss colors that match the felt on the front. Leave the top edge open.

4 Fold the stocking hanger piece in half to make a loop and stitch the ends to the backside of the stocking front, inside at the top left corner.

5 Position the gnome's beard over the face piece, and stitch them together using the stab stitch. Stitch one blue body piece in place behind the beard. Add one hat piece so it overlaps the face and beard, and stitch it in place.

6 To make the back of the gnome, line the second hat piece, hair (back side), and the second body piece so they match the front of the gnome. Sew these back pieces together just as you did with the front pieces, but don't stitch the front and back of the gnome together yet.

7 Add some embroidery to the front of the gnome. Use the dark brown floss to stitch the eyes using the satin stitch and the nose and mouth using the straight stitch. Use straight stitches and a lazy daisy with the green floss to decorate the hat.

8 Pin the front and back pieces of the gnome together, and stitch them around the outer edge using the whipstitch. When you have a 1-inch (2.5 cm) opening left, stuff the gnome with a bit of stuffing, and then sew up the hole. Tuck your little Santa Gnome into the pocket on the front of the stocking.

Ah, winter pleasures: catching the first snowflake on your tongue and a full stocking on Christmas morning!

Jolly Snowman Stocking

DESIGNER: KATHY SHELDON

WHAT YOU NEED

Basic sewing kit (page 7)

Templates (page 122)

Green felt, two 9 x 12-inch (22.9 x 30.5 cm) sheets

White felt, 9 x 12-inch (22.9 x 30.5 cm) sheet

Tiny red felt scrap

Gray, orange, white, brown, and green embroidery floss

Decorative ribbon, 7 inches (17.8 cm)

WHAT YOU DO

1 Using the templates, cut two stocking shapes from the green felt, the scalloped cuff from the white felt, and the tongue from the felt scrap (it might be easier to just cut the tiny tongue freehand).

2 Use the template and a disappearing or water-soluble fabric pen to trace the snowman's outline and features (except for the arms) onto the remaining white felt.

3 Hoop the felt and embroider the features onto the snowman. Use six strands of the gray floss and large French knots to make the buttons. Use two strands of gray floss and the backstitch for the eyes and the mouth. Use two strands of the orange floss and the backstitch for the carrot nose. Use two strands of the white floss to attach the felt tongue to the center of the mouth with a small French knot. Unhoop the felt.

4 Cut the outline of the embroidered snowman from the felt and pin it in place on the front stocking piece, using the photo as a guide. Use two strands of the white floss and the straight stitch to attach the snowman to the stocking front.

5 Either use the disappearing or water-soluble fabric pen to draw the stick arms onto the stocking freehand or trace the outline of the snowman and the arms onto tissue paper and pin it in place over the embroidered snowman. Use six strands of the brown floss and the stem stitch for the arms.

6 Use six strands of the white floss to make large French knots to sprinkle snowflakes onto the stocking.

7 Pin the white scalloped cuff to the stocking front, aligning the straight top with the top of the stocking. Starting on the right side, use the running stitch and six strands of the green floss to attach the cuff to the stocking, but stop stitching (without cutting or tying off the floss) about three-quarters of the way across the cuff.

8 Align the stocking back behind the front piece. Fold the decorative ribbon in half and pin it in place between the stocking pieces so that about 1¼ inches (3.2 cm) of ribbon ends are inside the stocking. Continue with the running stitch across the top of the cuff, catching the folded ribbon and sewing all the way through to the back of the stocking back to secure the ribbon hanger.

9 Use the blanket stitch and six strands of green floss around the outside edge of the stocking to secure the front to the back, stitching under the white cuff on both sides.

Add some Western flair to your holidays with this two-tone stocking.

Western Stocking

DESIGNER: JODIE RACKLEY

WHAT YOU NEED

Basic sewing kit (page 7)

Templates (page 129)

½ yard (.5 m) of gray felt

White felt, 9 x 12-inch (22.9 x 30.5 cm) sheet

White embroidery floss

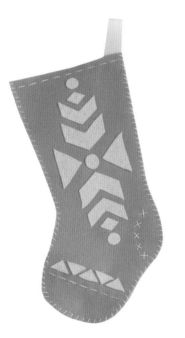

WHAT YOU DO

1 Use the templates to cut two stocking pieces from the gray felt and two large and small chevron pieces, two large triangles, two diamond shapes, two small circles, one larger circle, and five small triangles from the white felt. Cut out a 1 x 6-inch (2.5 x 15.2 cm) strip of white felt and set aside for step 6.

2 Line the five small triangle shapes across the toe of the stocking front. Pin or glue them in place, and make three small straight stitches in the shape of a triangle on each piece. Sew a running stitch in a line along the bottom of the triangles to further define the toe.

3 Using the photos as a guide, pin or glue the rest of the white shapes in place on the stocking front.

4 Starting with the center circle and the large triangles, use the straight stitch to sew all of the shapes in place.

5 Sew five cross stitches to define the heel of your stocking. Stitch a line of straight stitch along the top straight edge of the stocking front.

6 Fold the 1 x 6-inch (2.5 x 15.2 cm) strip of white felt in half and place it on the right top corner of your stocking back. Stitch it in place using a large cross stitch; this loop will be used for hanging the stocking.

7 Layer the stocking front and back pieces together, with wrong sides facing. Using a long piece of embroidery floss and starting at the top corner where the hanging loop is, begin whipstitching along the edge, working your way around the stocking and leaving the top edge open.

Enlarged, this caroling bird design would also look great sewn onto a pillow.

Caroling Bird Stocking

DESIGNER: LAURA HOWARD

WHAT YOU NEED

Basic sewing kit (page 7)

Templates (page 117)

Blue wool felt (or other sturdy felt), approximately 17 x 20 inches (43.2 x 50.8 cm)

Gray felt, 2½ x 3 inches (6.4 x 7.6 cm)

Black felt, 5½ x 7 inches (14 x 17.8 cm)

White felt, 2½ x 3 inches (6.4 x 7.6 cm)

Coral or red felt, 4 x 4½ inches (10.2 x 11.4 cm)

Matching sewing threads

Black and blue embroidery floss

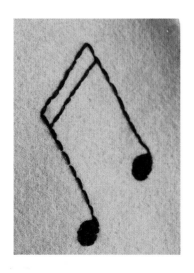

WHAT YOU DO

1 Use the templates provided to cut out all the felt pieces. Cut two stockings from blue felt; one bird, head, lower wing, pupil, and wing A from black felt; one eye, tail, and wing B from white felt; one wing C from gray felt; and one belly from coral or red felt.

2 Trace the musical notes onto white tissue paper, making sure to include the guideline in the top right corner. Pin this embroidery pattern to the stocking front, using the guideline to correctly position the pattern (see Tip).

TIP: To avoid sticking herself with the pins holding the tissue paper in place, Laura uses long tacking stitches to sew the tissue paper to the felt, removes the pins before embroidering, and then removes the tacking stitches before removing the tissue paper.

3 Using three strands of black floss and the backstitch, embroider the musical note design, taking care not to pull your stitches too tight and pucker the felt. Avoid carrying your floss between the notes to help keep the back of your work neat.

4 Carefully tear away the tissue paper to reveal your embroidery.

5 Use three stands of black floss, and satin stitch to fill in the ovals of the musical notes, as pictured. Again, avoid carrying your floss between the notes.

6 Position the black bird shape on the embroidered stocking and pin it in place. Use matching black sewing thread and small whipstitches to sew the shape to the backing felt.

7 Trace the legs embroidery pattern onto tissue paper and pin the pattern to the stocking so the bird's legs meet its belly (as pictured). Backstitch the legs with three stands of black floss. Remove the pins and carefully tear away the tissue paper.

8 Add the next layer of pieces to the bird one by one so they line up neatly with the black bird shape and with each other. Sew the black head, coral belly, white tail, and then the black lower wing piece by pinning each piece in position and then whipstitching it in place with matching sewing thread.

9 Sew the three wing pieces in place (wing A, B, and C) with more whipstitches and matching sewing threads.

Stockings & More

10 Position the eye and pupil using the photo as a guide and sew them with the whipstitch and matching sewing thread.

Optional: Sew a slightly curved line with black sewing thread to mark where the beak joins the bird's head. Sew a line of small black running stitches up and then back again to create a continuous line of stitching.

11 Cut two strips of blue felt measuring ¾ x 7 inches (1.9 x 17.8 cm) for the hanger. Pin the two strips together and use three strands of matching blue embroidery floss to blanket stitch the edges together. Leave the two narrow ends unstitched.

12 Fold the felt to form a loop and position it in the top right corner of the back stocking piece, so the loop overlaps the stocking by about an inch (2.5 cm). Leave enough room to blanket stitch the front and back of the stocking together later.

13 Use three strands of matching blue embroidery floss and stitch a rectangle to securely sew the ends of the loop to the stocking. Sew a line of running stitch in one direction then sew back along the line you've just sewn to create a continuous line of stitching. Turn the stocking back and forth as you sew to help keep your stitching neat.

14 Pin the front and back of the stocking together, with wrong sides facing. Trim any excess felt from the edge of the back stocking piece if necessary (embroidering the front piece may have caused it to shrink slightly). Blanket stitch the edges of the stocking together with three strands of matching blue embroidery floss, leaving the top edge of the stocking open.

Happy Elf Friends

DESIGNER: MOLLIE JOHANSON

These happy little elves will give you lots of holiday hugs!

Happy Elf Friends

WHAT YOU NEED

(to make the girl elf)

Basic sewing kit (page 7)

Templates (page 121)

Red felt, 11 x 12 inches (27.9 x 30.5 cm)

Light blue felt, 5 x 7 inches (12.7 x 17.8 cm)

Tan felt, 3 x 3 inches (7.6 x 7.6 cm)

Yellow felt, 2 x 3½ inches (5.1 x 8.9 cm)

Cotton print fabric, 8 x 11 inches (20.3 x 27.9 cm)

Brown, white, and yellow embroidery floss

Black plastic safety eyes

3 small jingle bells

Polyester stuffing

Note: If you'll be giving an elf to a young child, you should consider leaving off the jingle bells, plastic eyes, and buttons. Embroider the eyes and buttons instead.

Extra idea: To make the boy elf, as pictured on the previous page, use the curly hair and pocket templates and alternate felt and fabric colors. Mix up the colors and accessories for even more elf friends!

WHAT YOU DO

1 From red felt, cut out four arms, four legs, two hats, one collar, two buttons, one bow and one bow knot. From light blue felt, cut out two hat crown pieces. From tan felt, cut one face and two ears. From yellow felt, cut one straight hair and two pigtails. From the cotton print fabric, cut out two body pieces.

2 Embroider the nose and mouth onto the face piece using three strands of brown floss and the backstitch. Attach the face, ears, collar, and hair to one of the body pieces, layering the pieces and sewing with the straight stitch. Sew the felt buttons in place with Xs. You can use matching floss or contrasting colors.

3 If you're using plastic safety eyes, attach each eye by making a hole through the felt and fabric, pushing the eye post through the hole and pressing the washer on the back.

4 Stitch the matching arm and leg pieces together, sewing around the two felt pieces with the straight stitch and leaving the straight end open. Fill each arm and leg with a small amount of stuffing.

5 Place the front body piece right (print) side facing up. Machine baste the arms and legs to the fabric so they are facing in and the straight edges align with the edge of the fabric.

Be sure to fold in the tips of the ears so they don't get caught in the seams.

6 Pull the legs so they hang down from the body. Pin the back body piece in place on top of the arms so the front and back body pieces are aligned and right (print) sides together. It will be a little lumpy. Starting at the bottom corner, sew up the side, top, and down the other side, leaving the bottom open.

7 Clip the curves along the top, then turn the elf right side out. Fill the body with stuffing.

8 Pin the bottom edge together so that it has ¼ inch (6 mm) of fabric folded in along each edge. Sew the opening closed by hand or top stitch it with a sewing machine.

9 Make the hat by stitching the two hat pieces together along the sides with the straight stitch. Attach the hat crown pieces along the front and back of the opening using the straight stitch. Sew the bow onto the crown with a few stitches on the layered center.

10 Stitch the jingle bells securely onto the tips of the feet and the hat. Slide the hat onto your elf's head, and she's ready to help Santa!

'Tis the season to drink toasty drinks,
and every hot mug needs a nice coaster.
To make this four coaster set use
 two coordinating colorways
and flip the mug templates
so you've got two pairs
facing in opposite directions.

Cocoa Coasters

DESIGNER: LAURA HOWARD

WHAT YOU NEED

(to make the set of 4 coasters shown)

Basic sewing kit (page 7)

Templates (page 117)

Lilac, purple, baby blue, blue, and dark brown felt

Felt scraps in white and pink

Lilac and baby blue embroidery floss

Matching sewing threads

TIP: Decorating the front of the coaster may cause the felt to shrink slightly. If so, finish your coaster by trimming any excess felt from the bottom layer.

WHAT YOU DO

To make each coaster

1 Use the templates provided to cut out the following pieces: one mug and mug front (color A), one small circle (color B), two large circles (color C), one cocoa (dark brown), and three marshmallows (a mix of pink and white). When cutting out the mug, cut along the dotted line to access and cut out the inside of the handle (this will be sewn up again later).

2 Place the small circle in the center of one of the large circles and pin it in place. Using three strands of embroidery floss to match the mug (color A), sew a line of backstitch just inside the small circle, joining the two layers of felt together.

3 Position the mug piece in the center of the coaster and arrange the mug front and cocoa pieces on top of it so they line up neatly. Pin and then sew them in position with the whipstitch and matching sewing threads. As you sew the handle, remember to whipstitch along where you cut in step 1.

4 Add the marshmallows one by one. If you're making a set of coasters you can vary the position of the marshmallows,

as pictured. Sew them in place with the whipstitch and matching pink and white sewing threads.

5 Place the decorated coaster on top of the remaining large circle. Use sewing thread to match the large circles (color C) and sew a line of running stitch flush with the edge of the small circle so your stitching is hidden.

You won't mind getting the sniffles when it means reaching for this gingerbread house filled with tissues. They pop right through the ridge of the candy-covered roof!

Gingerbread House Tissue Box Cover

DESIGNER: MOLLIE JOHANSON

WHAT YOU NEED

Basic sewing kit (page 7)

Templates (page 120)

Tan felt, 12 x 18 inches (30.5 x 45.7 cm)

Pink felt, 6 x 8 inches (15.2 x 20.3 cm)

White felt, 6 x 8 inches (15.2 x 20.3 cm)

Felt scraps in various candy colors

White embroidery floss

WHAT YOU DO

1 Use the templates to cut all of the felt pieces. From tan felt, cut side panels A and B twice (for four panels total), a door, a window, and a gingerbread man. From the pink felt, cut four roof piece A sections, and from the white felt, cut four roof piece B sections. Cut additional candy pieces from the other colors, choosing as many as you want.

2 The roof consists of the folded tops of the A side panels covered with the scalloped pink and white roof pieces. To make the roof, first fold each side panel A piece down 3 inches (7.6 cm) at the top. Press the fold with an iron to crease. Working in the 3-inch (7.6 cm) creased section, pin a roof piece B so that the scallops extend over the crease. Stitch along the top with three strands of embroidery floss and the straight stitch. Layer and pin a roof piece A over the first roof piece and stitch along the top. Add two more roof pieces, evenly spacing them and ending with a roof piece A aligned with the top edge. Repeat with the second side panel A.

3 Using three strands of embroidery floss, stitch the details onto the door, window, and gingerbread man. Use French knots for the eyes, the scallop stitch for the mouths, the backstitch for the door knob and gingerbread buttons, and the straight stitch for the window panes.

4 Attach the door, window, gingerbread man, and all the candies you like to the side panels of the house with the straight stitch. Stitch the lollipop sticks and extra details with the straight stitch.

5 Holding one side panel A to a side panel B with wrong sides together, stitch along the side with three strands of white floss and the straight stitch, using a 1/8-inch (3 mm) seam allowance. Sew the side of the roof to the angled portion of the side panel B, stitching through the scalloped roof pieces. Repeat for each corner of the house.

6 Slide the gingerbread house over a box of tissues and pull the first tissue through the open top of the roof.

No time to stitch? These handsome holly tags are no sew, and the gift card sleeve requires only that you sew on two buttons!

Holly Gift Tags & Gift Card Sleeve

DESIGNER: JENNIFER JESSEE

no sew

WHAT YOU NEED

(to make the gift tags)

Basic sewing kit (page 7)

Templates (page 121)

Felt scraps in white, dark green, light green, dark pink, light pink, and medium pink

2½ x 5-inch (6.4 x 12.7 cm) craft tags with pre-punched hole

Baker's twine

Fabric glue

(to make the gift card sleeve)

Basic sewing kit (page 7)

Templates (page 121)

6¾ x 4½-inch (17.1 x 11.4 cm) rectangle of light green felt

Felt scraps in white, dark green, light green, dark pink, and medium pink

Two matching buttons

Green embroidery floss

Baker's twine

Fabric glue

WHAT YOU DO

To make the gift tags

1 Using the templates, cut one background shape, each side of the leaf, and two or three berries in the colors of your choice.

2 Glue these onto the front of the tag, starting with the oval-like background shape, followed by the leaves and berries.

3 Cut a 9-inch (22.9 cm) length of baker's twine, and tie the ends together. Feed this end through the hole to create a loop.

To make the gift card sleeve

1 Fold the bottom half of the light green rectangle up 2¾ inches (7 cm). Keeping the sides aligned, iron across the bottom to create a crease.

2 Fold the top of the felt down 1¼ inches (3.2 cm), and iron to create a top crease to create a closure flap for your sleeve.

3 Glue the left and right side of the bottom flap to the layer under it, working about ¼ inch (1.6 mm) from the outside edge and leaving enough area for a gift card to slide in. Be sure not to get any glue on the closure flap. Let the sleeve fully dry.

4 With the sleeve closed, trim the left and right side edges with pinking shears or scallop fabric shears.

5 Using the templates, cut one background shape, each side of the leaf, and two or three berries in the colors of your choice. Glue these onto the front of the sleeve, starting with the oval-like background shape and then the leaves and berries. Let dry.

6 Using three strands of green embroidery floss, sew the buttons to the back of the sleeve, centering them and placing one on the closure flap and one on the bottom flap.

7 Cut an 11-inch (27.9 cm) piece of bakery twine and thread it onto a needle. Tie a knot at the end, thread the strand, and stitch up from underneath the closure flap, coming out from underneath the top button. Remove the needle and tie a knot in the end of the twine so it won't unravel. Wrap the twine in a figure 8 shape from button to button to close the flap.

This little polar cub will bring
a smile to everyone's face on
Christmas morning.

Polar Bear Gift Bag

DESIGNER: KATHY SHELDON

WHAT YOU NEED

Basic sewing kit (page 7)

Templates (page 125)

Red stiffened felt, 12 x 18-inch (30.5 cm x 45.7 cm) sheet

White felt, 2½-inch (6.4 cm) square

Blue felt, 9 x 12-inch (22.9 x 30.5 cm) sheet*

White, black, and red embroidery floss

***Note:** You only need enough blue felt to cut a 3-inch-diameter (7.6 cm) circle, but if you start with a larger piece, you can hoop the felt to make attaching the polar bear and embroidering the details easier.

WHAT YOU DO

1 Using the templates, cut two bag sides and one bottom from the stiffened red felt and the polar bear outline from the white felt. Don't cut the blue appliqué circle yet.

2 Insert the blue felt into the embroidery hoop and the pin the polar bear in the center. Use the straight stitch and one strand of white floss along the outside edge of the bear to attach the bear to the blue felt. When you get to the right ear, stitch a little curve slightly inside the ear; when you get to the left ear, leave the top of the ear free, and stitch a straight line across the bottom of that ear to delineate the edge of the head.

3 Trace the polar bear, including the eyes, nose, and mouth, onto a piece of tissue or tracing paper and cut around it roughly. Pin the tissue paper onto the felt polar bear.

4 Use close straight stitches or the backstitch and four strands of white floss to add the lines to delineate the bear's legs. Use one strand of black floss and the satin stitch to stitch the nose and the right eye. The left eye is simply one short vertical stitch and the mouth is a slightly longer diagonal stitch. Carefully remove the tissue or tracing paper,

using the embroidery needle or tweezers to remove any paper that's stuck.

5 Use one strand of the white floss and the star stitch to add snowflakes in a random pattern around the top of the bear. Remove the felt from the hoop.

6 Center the appliqué circle template over the embroidered bear and stars. Trace the circle onto the fabric with a disappearing or water-soluble fabric pen. Cut the circle from the felt.

7 Position the appliqué circle on the outside of the bag's front piece, using the photo as a guide, and pin it in place. Use three strands of the red floss and the straight stitch around the outside edge of the circle to secure the circle to the front piece. Remove the pins.

8 Align the back and front bag pieces with the embellished front facing out. Whipstitch the two sides of the pieces together with three strands of red floss.

9 Whipstitch the bottom circle in place using three strands of red floss.

10 Use the blanket stitch and six strands of white floss to add a decorative trim along the top of the gift bag.

TEMPLATES

See page 8 for more on transferring templates and embroidery designs.

TIP: For projects that require templates to be photocopied at 400%, try copying the template once at 200% and then copy the photocopy of the template at 200%. Your final photocopied template will be 400%.

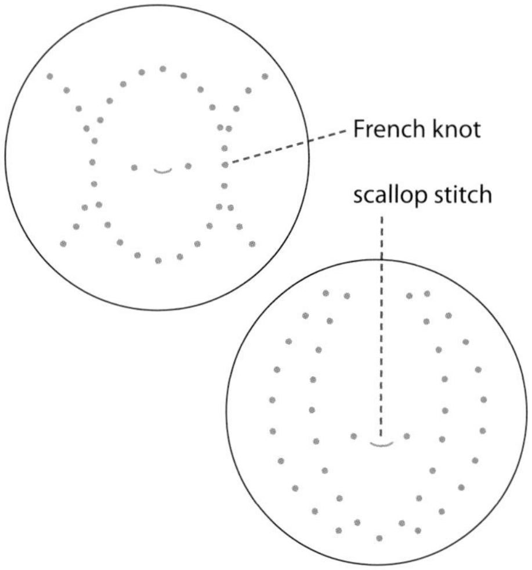

ARGYLE FOX
Page 14 — copy at 200%

BEADED STAR BAUBLES
Page 16 — copy at 200%

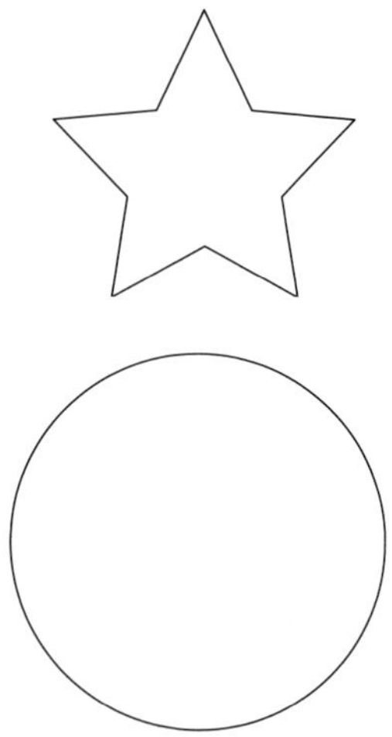

CLOVE-FILLED ORANGE POMANDER ORNAMENTS
Page 18 — copy at 200%

French knot

scallop stitch

(cut 2)

BIRD MOBILE
Page 52 — copy at 200%

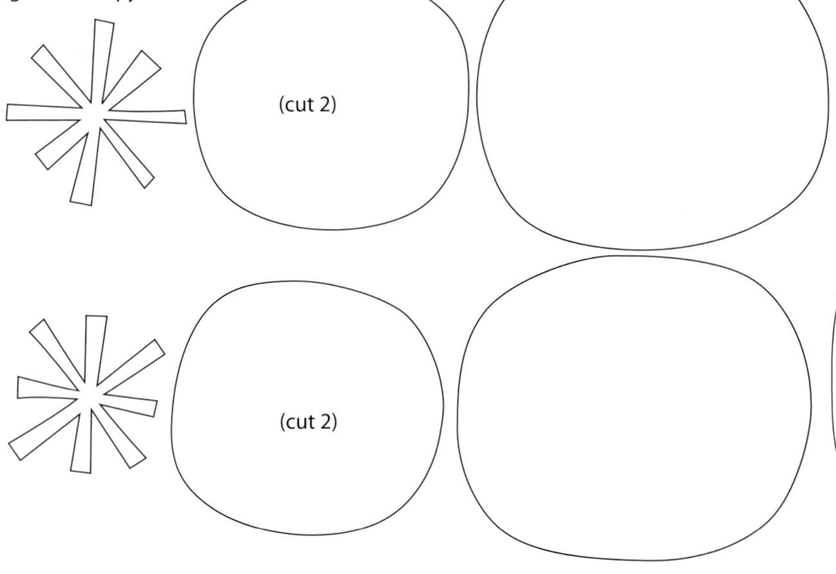

(cut 2)

(cut 2)

(cut 2)

beak

CAROLING BIRD STOCKING
Page 102 — copy at 400%

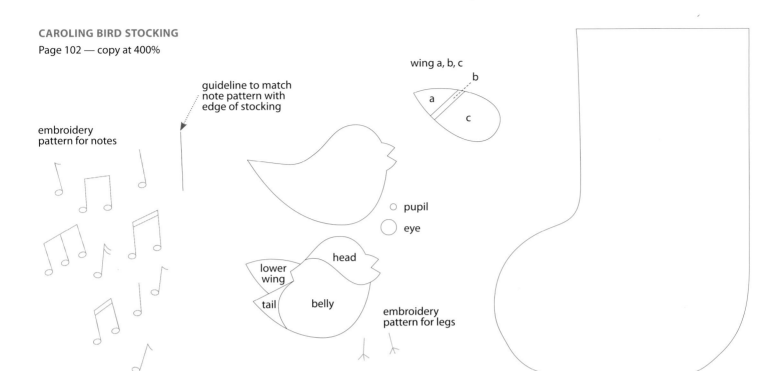

embroidery
pattern for notes

guideline to match
note pattern with
edge of stocking

wing a, b, c

a

b

c

pupil

eye

head

lower
wing

tail

belly

embroidery
pattern for legs

CHRISTMAS IS COMING WREATH MAT
Page 54 — copy at 400%

COCOA COASTERS
PAGE 108 — COPY AT 200%

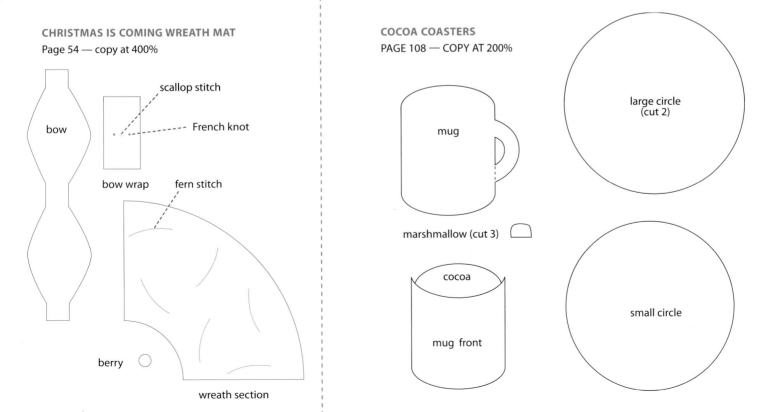

bow

scallop stitch

French knot

bow wrap

fern stitch

berry

wreath section

mug

marshmallow (cut 3)

cocoa

mug front

large circle
(cut 2)

small circle

DALA HORSE ORNAMENT
Page 20 — copy at 200%

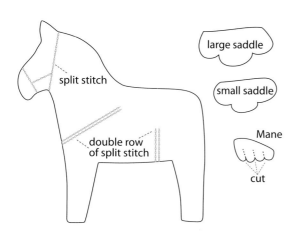

split stitch

double row
of split stitch

large saddle

small saddle

Mane

cut

DANGLING STARS ORNAMENTS
Page 56 — copy at 200%

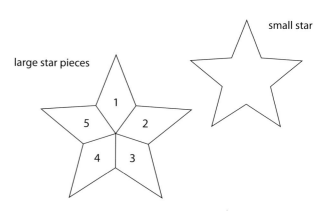

small star

large star pieces

1

5

2

4

3

DOVE ORNAMENTS
Page 22 — copy at 200%

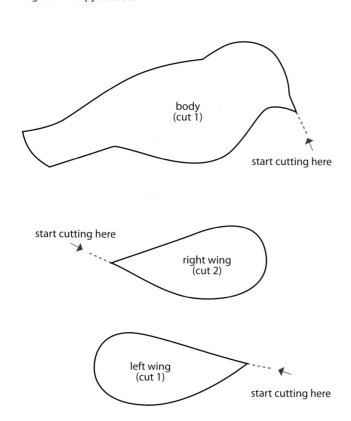

body
(cut 1)

start cutting here

start cutting here

right wing
(cut 2)

left wing
(cut 1)

start cutting here

EASY TREE GARLAND
Page 58 — copy at 100%

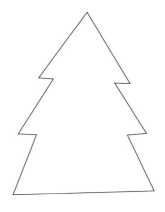

FA LA LA LA LLAMA
Page 24 — copy at 200%

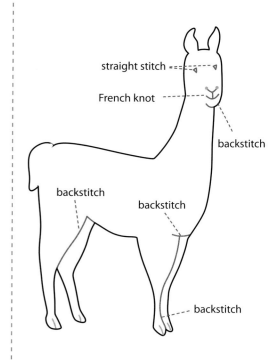

straight stitch

French knot

backstitch

backstitch

backstitch

backstitch

FELT & FABRIC TREES
Page 60 — copy at 400%

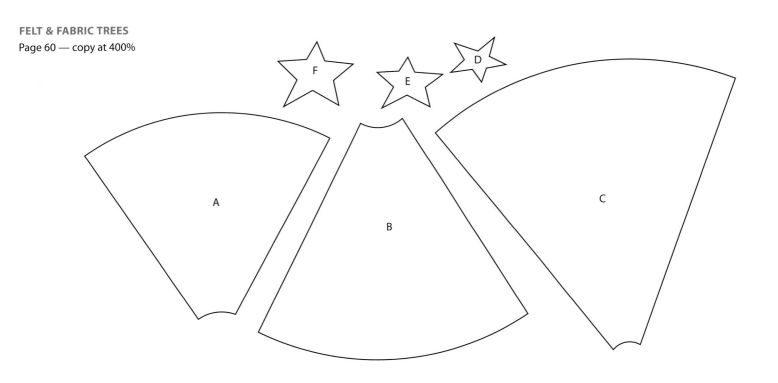

FELT LIGHT UP VILLAGE
Page 64 — copy at 200%

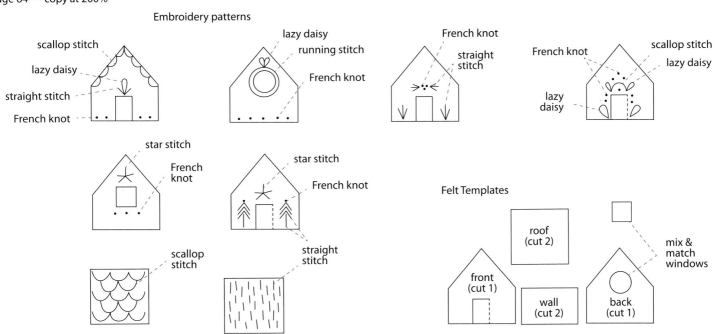

Embroidery patterns

scallop stitch
lazy daisy
straight stitch
French knot

lazy daisy
running stitch
French knot

French knot
straight stitch

French knot
scallop stitch
lazy daisy
lazy daisy

star stitch
French knot

star stitch
French knot
straight stitch

scallop stitch

straight stitch

Felt Templates

roof (cut 2)

front (cut 1)

wall (cut 2)

back (cut 1)

mix & match windows

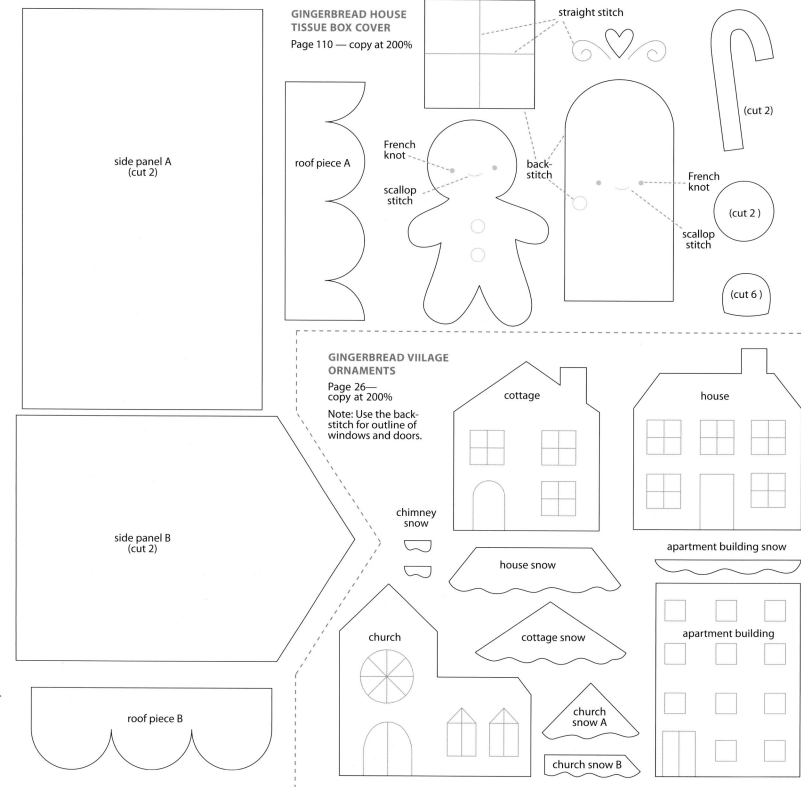

GINGERBREAD HOUSE TISSUE BOX COVER

Page 110 — copy at 200%

straight stitch

side panel A
(cut 2)

roof piece A

French knot

scallop stitch

back-stitch

French knot

scallop stitch

(cut 2)

(cut 2)

(cut 6)

GINGERBREAD VIILAGE ORNAMENTS

Page 26—
copy at 200%

Note: Use the back-stitch for outline of windows and doors.

cottage

house

chimney snow

house snow

apartment building snow

side panel B
(cut 2)

church

cottage snow

apartment building

church snow A

church snow B

roof piece B

HAPPY ELF FRIENDS
Page 105 — copy at 200%

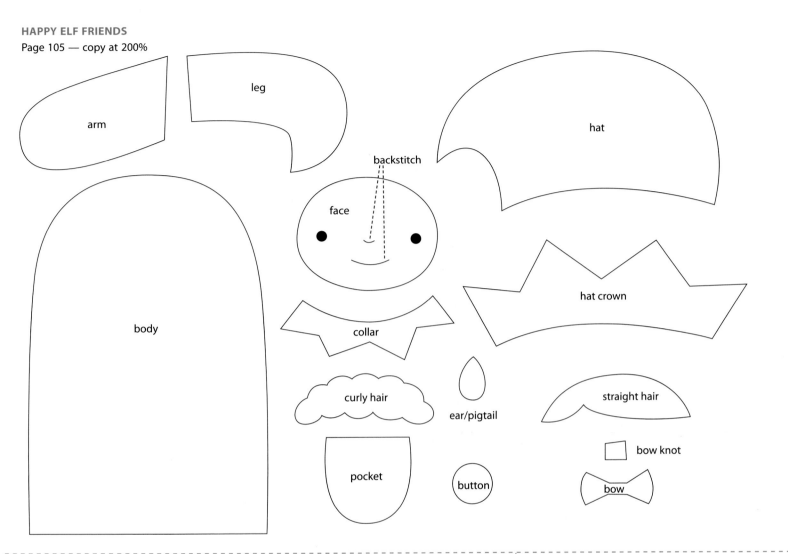

arm

leg

hat

backstitch

face

hat crown

body

collar

curly hair

ear/pigtail

straight hair

bow knot

pocket

button

bow

HOLLY GIFT TAGS & GIFT CARD SLEEVE
Page 112 — copy at 200%

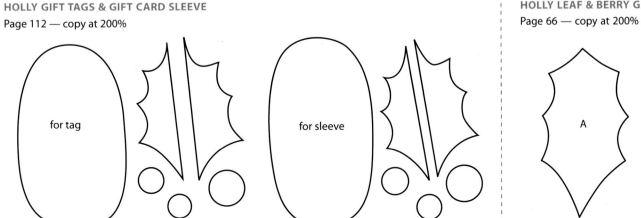

for tag

for sleeve

HOLLY LEAF & BERRY GARLAND
Page 66 — copy at 200%

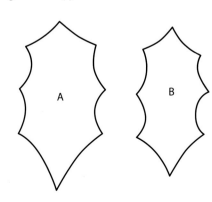

A

B

Templates

HOOPED REINDEER

Page 68 —
copy at 100%

JOLLY SNOWMAN STOCKING

Page 98 — copy at 200%

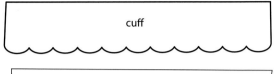

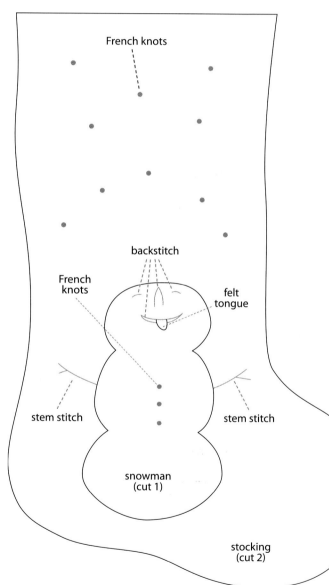

cuff

French knots

backstitch

French
knots

felt
tongue

stem stitch

stem stitch

snowman
(cut 1)

stocking
(cut 2)

JOY TO THE WORLD GARLAND

Page 70 — copy at 200%

JOY
TO THE
WORLD!

KOOL KRISTMAS KITTY
Page 28 — copy at 200%

pupils

bow pieces

cut 1 pink   cut 1 blue

eye   eye

nose

ear   ear

face

body

MISTLETOE SPRIG
Page 74 — copy at 200%

MINI GIFTS GARLAND
Page 72 — copy at 200%

large ribbon

large gift

bow

center circle

small ribbon

small gift

left ribbon

right ribbon

PARTRIDGE & PEARS ORNAMENTS
Page 30 — copy at 200%

beak

face

wing

body

belly

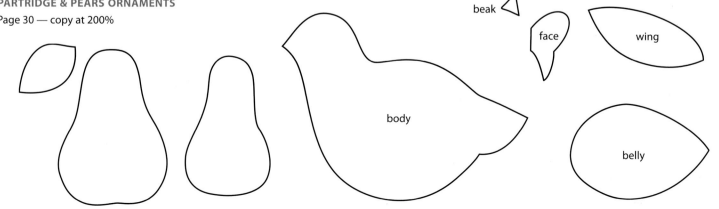

Templates

PINK, GOLD & GRAY ORNAMENT TRIO
Page 33 — copy at 200%

Bird Ornament

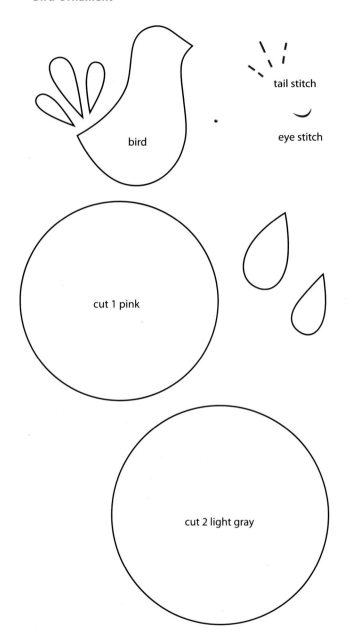

tail stitch

eye stitch

bird

cut 1 pink

cut 2 light gray

Bauble Ornament

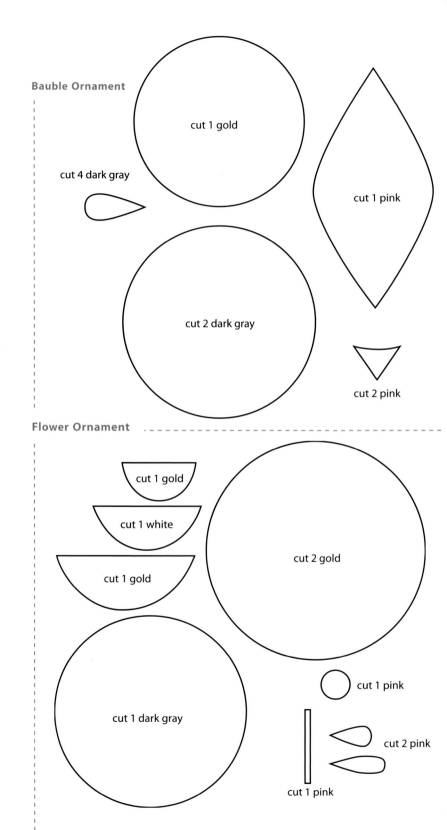

cut 1 gold

cut 4 dark gray

cut 1 pink

cut 2 dark gray

cut 2 pink

Flower Ornament

cut 1 gold

cut 1 white

cut 1 gold

cut 2 gold

cut 1 dark gray

cut 1 pink

cut 2 pink

cut 1 pink

• 'Tis the Season to Be Felt-y

POLAR BEAR GIFT BAG

Page 114 — copy Polar Bear appliqué patch and bag bottom at 100%

Page 114 — copy bag sides at 200%

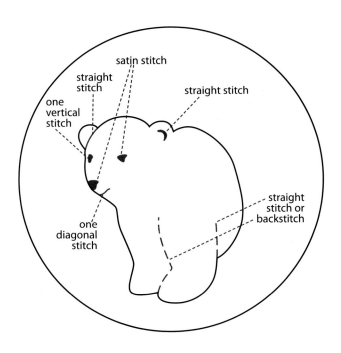

satin stitch

straight stitch

straight stitch

one vertical stitch

one diagonal stitch

straight stitch or backstitch

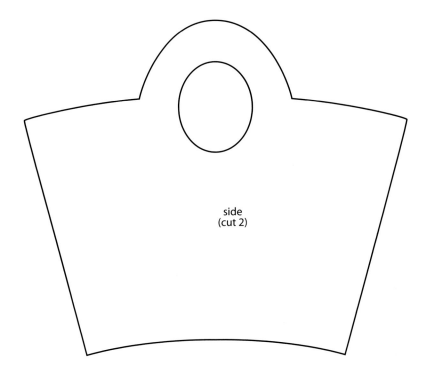

side (cut 2)

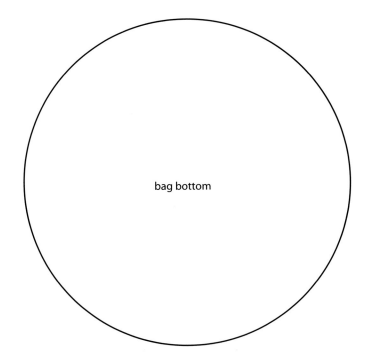

bag bottom

PRETTY IN PINK POINTSETTIA WREATH

Page 76 copy at 100%

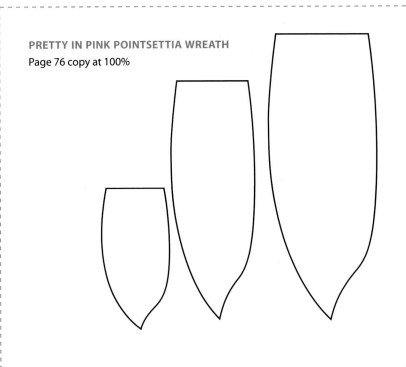

RAINBOW STAR STOCKING
Page 94 — copy at 400%

A stars   B stars

RING MY BELLS GARLAND
Page 82 — copy at 200%

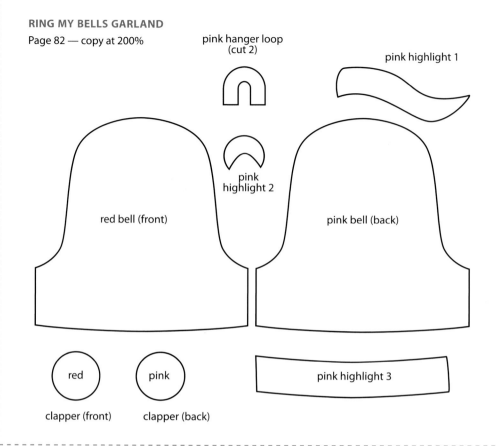

pink hanger loop
(cut 2)

pink highlight 1

red bell (front)

pink bell (back)

pink
highlight 2

pink highlight 3

red

pink

clapper (front)   clapper (back)

RUSTIC REINDEER
Page 79 — copy at 200%

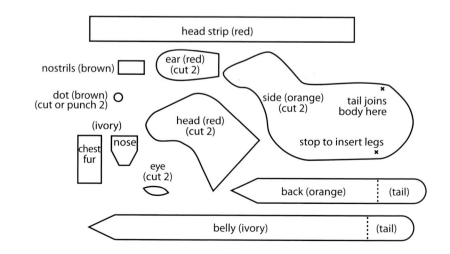

head strip (red)

nostrils (brown)

ear (red)
(cut 2)

dot (brown)
(cut or punch 2)

side (orange)
(cut 2)

tail joins
body here

(ivory)

head (red)
(cut 2)

stop to insert legs

chest
fur

nose

eye
(cut 2)

back (orange)   (tail)

belly (ivory)   (tail)

SANTA GNOME STOCKING

Page 96 — copy at 200%

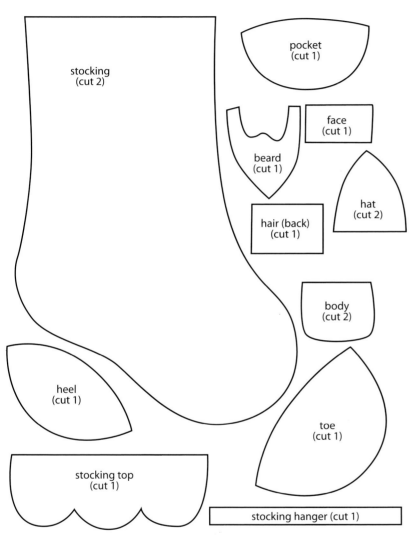

stocking
(cut 2)

pocket
(cut 1)

face
(cut 1)

beard
(cut 1)

hat
(cut 2)

hair (back)
(cut 1)

body
(cut 2)

heel
(cut 1)

toe
(cut 1)

stocking top
(cut 1)

stocking hanger (cut 1)

SHINNING STAR TREE TOPPER

Page 36 — copy at 200%

backstitch with beads

SCRAPPY WREATH

Page 84 — copy at 100%

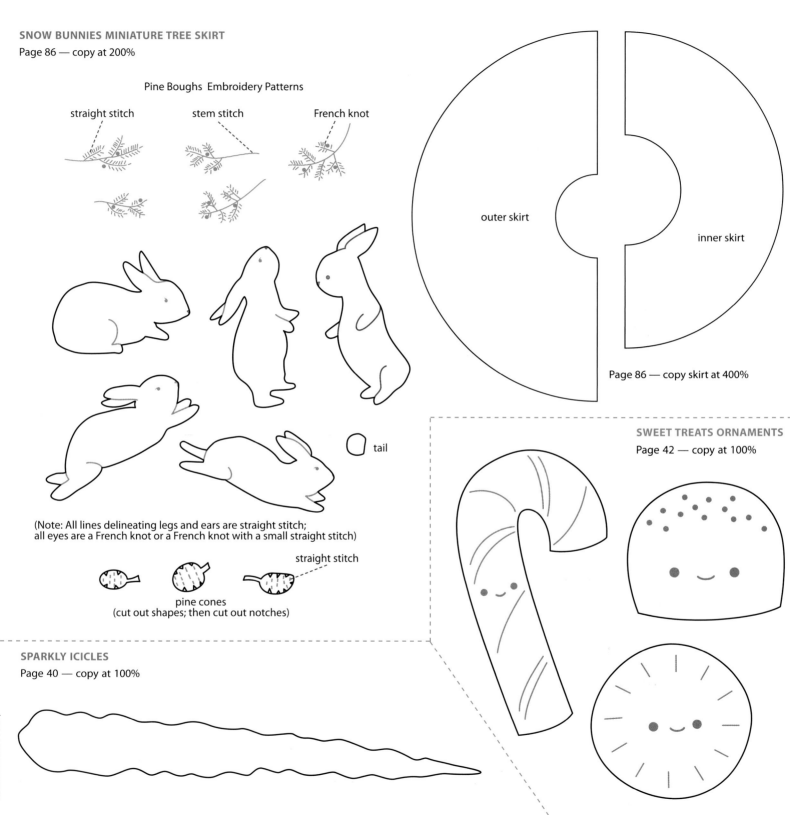

SNOW BUNNIES MINIATURE TREE SKIRT
Page 86 — copy at 200%

Pine Boughs Embroidery Patterns

straight stitch   stem stitch   French knot

outer skirt

inner skirt

Page 86 — copy skirt at 400%

tail

(Note: All lines delineating legs and ears are straight stitch;
all eyes are a French knot or a French knot with a small straight stitch)

straight stitch

pine cones
(cut out shapes; then cut out notches)

SWEET TREATS ORNAMENTS
Page 42 — copy at 100%

SPARKLY ICICLES
Page 40 — copy at 100%

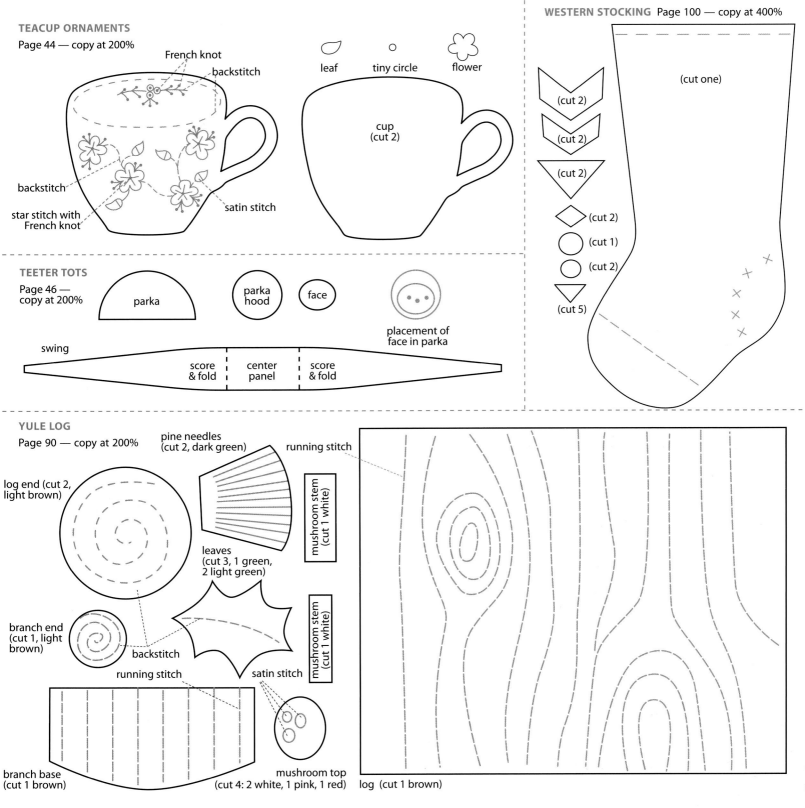

TEACUP ORNAMENTS
Page 44 — copy at 200%

French knot

backstitch

leaf   tiny circle   flower

backstitch

cup
(cut 2)

star stitch with
French knot

satin stitch

TEETER TOTS
Page 46 —
copy at 200%

parka

parka
hood

face

placement of
face in parka

swing

score
& fold

center
panel

score
& fold

WESTERN STOCKING Page 100 — copy at 400%

(cut one)

(cut 2)

(cut 2)

(cut 2)

(cut 2)

(cut 1)

(cut 2)

(cut 5)

YULE LOG

Page 90 — copy at 200%

pine needles
(cut 2, dark green)

running stitch

log end (cut 2,
light brown)

mushroom stem
(cut 1 white)

leaves
(cut 3, 1 green,
2 light green)

mushroom stem
(cut 1 white)

branch end
(cut 1, light
brown)

backstitch

running stitch

satin stitch

branch base
(cut 1 brown)

mushroom top
(cut 4: 2 white, 1 pink, 1 red)

log (cut 1 brown)

A B O U T *the* D E S I G N E R S

LAURA HOWARD

Laura is a designer, crafter, and author who likes to make and do . . . and is completely obsessed with felt! She's the author of two books about felt crafting: *Super-Cute Felt* and *Super-Cute Felt Animals*. Laura shares free tutorials and writes about her crafty adventures on her blog www.bugsandfishes.blogspot.com and sells her work at www.lupin.bigcartel.com.

JENNIFER JESSEE

Inspired by vintage fabrics, magazines, and cookbooks, Jennifer Jessee has been creating fun, stylish, retro designs for more than 25 years. Her illustration work can be found in a wide variety of publications in the United States and abroad, including *Wired*, *Spin*, *Mademoiselle*, and *Atlantic Monthly*. She learned to cross stitch at the age of nine with the help of her grandmother. Working with felt was a new, exciting medium for Jennifer, and now she's looking forward to felt finding its way into her collage and illustration pieces. You can find Jennifer's work at jenniferjessee.com.

MOLLIE JOHANSON

Mollie Johanson has loved creating and crafting cute things for as long as she can remember. She is the author of *Stitch Love: Sweet Creatures Big & Small* (Lark, 2015), and contributed to *Heart-Felt Holidays* (Lark, 2012), and *Felt-o-ween* (Lark, 2014), as well as other Lark Craft titles. Mollie lives near Chicago and is happiest with a cup of coffee, some stitching, and her family close at hand. Visit her at molliejohanson.com.

LISA JORDAN

Lisa Jordan is an artist living in rural Minnesota. Prone to tinkering with wood and wool, she's deeply inspired by nature and expresses her love of the odd and often overlooked bits of it through her work. She can be found blogging about her work and life out in the woods at www.lilfishstudios.com.

SUZIE MILLIONS

Suzie Millions is a cat-loving, vintage dress–wearing artist and compulsive crafter who lives with her musician/letterpress printer husband, Lance, in a swinging '50s house in scenic Asheville, North Carolina. Her craft opus, *The Complete Book of Retro Crafts*, was published by Lark in 2008, and she's a frequent contributor to other Lark books (her Felty Family Portraits from *Heart-Felt Holidays* are featured on Martha Stewart's Living blog). Visit her at www.Suziemillions.com and www.pinterest.com/retrosuzie.

JODIE RACKLEY

Jodie Rackley is the crafter and designer of Lova Revolutionary, a line of hand-stitched eco felt and embroidery gifts that can be found at lovely boutiques across the country and online at Etsy. She is the author of *Happy Stitch: 30 Felt and Fabric Projects for Everyday*. Her work as been featured in *Crafty* magazine and *Mollie Makes* and at the Craft and Hobby Association Trade Show as a featured artist for Kunin Eco Felt. Jodie is currently working on a line of embroidery and felt craft patterns for her Etsy shop (Lovahandmade.etsy.com). Keep up with her crafting at Lovarevolutionary.blogspot.com.

AIMEE RAY

Aimee Ray loves all types of art and crafts and is always trying something new. Besides embroidery, she dabbles in illustration, crochet, needle felting, sewing, and doll customizing. Aimee is the author of *Doodle Stitching* (Lark, 2007), *Doodle Stitching: The Motif Collection*, (Lark, 2010), *Doodle Stitching: Embroidery & Beyond* (Lark, 2013), and *Doodle Stitching: The Holiday Motif Collection* (Lark, 2014), and is the co-author with Kathy Sheldon of a book on making jewelry: *Aimee Ray's Sweet & Simple Jewelry* (Lark, 2013). In addition, she has contributed to many other Lark titles. You can see more of her work at www.dreamfollow.com and follow her daily crafting endeavors at www.littledeartracks.blogspot.com.

CYNTHIA SHAFFER

Cynthia Shaffer is a quilter, creative sewer, and photographer. Numerous books and magazines have featured Cynthia's art and photography work: she is the author of *Stash Happy Patchwork* (Lark, 2011), *Stash Happy Appliqué* (Lark, 2012), and *Coastal Crafts* (Lark, 2015), and co-author of *Serge It* (Lark, 2014). In her spare time Cynthia knits, paints, dabbles in mixed media art, and can be found every day at the gym, kick boxing. Cynthia lives with her husband Scott, sons Corry and Cameron, and beloved dogs Harper and Berklee in Southern California. For more information visit Cynthia online at cynthiashaffer.typepad.com or www.cynthiashaffer.com.

CHRISTI WHITELEY

Christi owns and operates Eldorado Mid Century Salvage antique business in Asheville, North Carolina, with her husband, Simon. She is also an interior designer, photo stylist, artist, and former fashion designer. See more of what Christi is up to at her Etsy shop (etsy.com/shop/EldoradoModern).

A B O U T *the* A U T H O R S

KATHY SHELDON

Kathy Sheldon writes, edits, and packages books. She grew up on a farm in New England, so making things by hand comes naturally to her. She's happiest when creating, whether it's a shrink plastic bracelet, a poem, a row of sweet peas, or a book about gardening or crafts. She is the author of many books, including *Shrink! Shrank! Shrunk!: Making Shrink Plastic Jewelry* (Lark, 2012), and the coauthor of *Fa la la la Felt!* (Lark, 2010), *Heart-Felt Holidays* (Lark, 2012), *Felt-o-ween* (Lark, 2014), and *Aimee Ray's Sweet & Simple Jewelry* (Lark, 2013). When Kathy is not writing or creating in the mountains of Asheville, North Carolina, you can usually find her at her cottage in Maine, where she's the first to jump in the lake in the spring and the last one to leave the water in the fall.

AMANDA CARESTIO

Amanda's latest crafting obsessions include crocheted hats, half-square triangles, and (still) fusible web. When she's not bent over her sewing machine, at the craft store, or exploring the Blue Ridge Mountains, Amanda enjoys spending quality time with her hubby, her sweet, sweet little girl, Miss Ruby, her soon-to-come baby boy, and her little brindle shadow, Violet. Amanda is the author of *Wee Felt Worlds* (Lark, 2013) and *Never Been Stitched* (Lark, 2014) (and other titles from Lark Crafts), and co-author of *Fa La La La Felt* (Lark, 2010), *Heart-Felt Holidays* (Lark, 2012) and *Felt-o-ween* (Lark, 2014). Her designs appear in many Lark Books.

Index